The Grammar Workbook

The Grammar Workbook

A SELF-STUDY GUIDE
FOR BUSINESS WRITERS

Paul Brollo

First published 1999 by
The Industrial Society
Robert Hyde House
48 Bryanston Square
London W1H 2EA

© The industrial Society 1999
Reprinted 2000, 2002

ISBN 1 85835 595 8
5787JC2.02

British Library Cataloguing-in-Publication Data.
A catalogue record for this book is available from the
British Library.

Typeset by: Wyvern 21 Ltd

Printed by: Cromwell Press

Cover design: Sign Design

The Industrial Society is a Registered Charity No. 290003

Contents

Introduction

The need to be in control of our writing

We are competing for time and energy when we communicate with each other in today's business world. We are all overloaded with information. Attention is concentration and concentration is energy and we need our energy to balance our busy lives. We have little or no time to process meaning. Consequently, we want clear and immediate messages from other people all the time. Furthermore, clear and direct messages are essential to success in our growing world of cross-cultural business.

Users rather than readers

We tend *to use* business documents rather than *to read* business documents because of our time and workload pressure. Consequently, I will write about *users* in The Workbook rather than *readers*. Writers who are in control of their writing make *using* a business document easier. As a result, others can make business decisions more effectively.

The user, the purpose, and the message of our writing

Communication is creating understanding in the minds of others to inform and to create action. We are responsible as writers for creating that understanding. Consequently, we need to be clear in our own minds about what is our message to our users. We also need to be clear about how we are going to support that message. Furthermore, we need to know our users as well as we possibly can know a business associate. Knowing our users will help us to present our message in such a way that our user will accept what we have to say. Finally, we need to be clear as to what outcome we want from our writing. We need a clear outcome so that we can measure how effectively we have communicated our message.

The relationship between thinking and writing

A relationship exists between thinking, writing, reading, and understanding. We have established above that having clear *guiding principles* is essential in order to write effectively. In other words, we need to establish our user, our purpose, and our message before we start writing. Clear writing is the result of clear thinking. Consequently, clear writing is the mark of a clear thinker. We can see writing as an objective way of displaying the shape of our thinking to others. As a result, good writing can be an aid to our personal and professional development.

Using a knowledge of grammar to control our writing

We place ourselves in a better position to control our writing if we equip ourselves with an awareness of grammar. Grammar reflects the distinctions which we make in the world around us and how we communicate those distinctions to other people. Grammar is a window into how our minds make sense of the world to themselves and to other people. Consequently, we can use our awareness of grammar to establish and present our messages clearly and unambiguously. We then can support our messages with carefully-structured and relevant material.

The route of acquisition

Furthermore, I have chosen to follow more or less the *route of acquisition* in The Workbook. The route of acquisition is the order in which we learn our first or any subsequent language. As a result, we will begin by exploring words; we will continue by exploring sentences; and we will conclude with paragraphs, punctuation, and style and tone. I have chosen a comprehensive approach to grammar in The Workbook. Nevertheless, I have tried to make grammar accessible through the use of clear explanations.

Appropriate style in business writing

Elements of style are often controversial in business writing. However, I have chosen to approach business writing from the point of view of *appropriateness* rather than *correctness*. An appropriate business style is a style which allows a writer to achieve the purpose of his or her document. We create the style of our writing through our use of grammar and vocabulary. Consequently, a writer who is aware of the rules of grammar is in a better position to control his or her style. Furthermore, a writer who is in control of his or her style is a writer in control of his or her message.

Who should use The Workbook

I have designed The Workbook for business writers at all levels. I have graded the material to help you to progress in the degree of your control over your writing. Consequently, you need to establish your own starting point according to your needs and objectives. You can use The Workbook in your own time and space either by yourself or with other people. Read *How To Use This Book* to find your own means to creating the solutions to your writing problems.

How to use
The Workbook

The structure of The Workbook

The Workbook follows the route by which we construct information to present to other people. This route is the same route which we use to learn a language. We call this route *the route of acquisition*. We will begin with the individual types of words. Next, we will look at how we form words into groups such as sentences. Finally, we will look at how we form sentences into paragraphs and at how we bind paragraphs with punctuation. Words, sentences, and paragraphs form the basis of all written texts.

The structure of each chapter

Each part of The Workbook will explain the relevant grammar point briefly. A series of exercises will follow each explanation. These exercises will allow you to put the relevant grammar point into practice. The exercises will be in the form of three grades: *essential exercises*, *bridging exercises*, and *applied exercises*. However, some grammar points have only a *general exercise*. Furthermore, other grammar points have no exercises since the information is for your reference only.

The exercises will provide three routes through the learning material and you could chose to follow one grade throughout The Workbook. However, I have designed the exercises to encourage you to go beyond your current state of knowledge.

The design of The Workbook

The Workbook is primarily a practical learning tool. Consequently, I have designed the reference sections so that you can scan these sections rapidly. I have used short blocks of information and subheadings throughout The Workbook. I have put also all the grammar and language terms in the *Glossary*. The *Glossary* is in the *Appendices*. You can scan the *Glossary* to find both the gaps in your knowledge and to consolidate your learning. Furthermore, I have put all the examples into *italics*. I have put the relevant grammar point within an example in **emboldened italics**.

I designed The Workbook for you to use as a learning tool and as a reference book rather than as a book for you to read. Consequently, you will find that I have repeated some of the information in different sections of The Workbook so that each section is as *self-contained* as possible.

The connections between the material

Areas of grammar tend to connect with each other and so we can visualise grammar as a *map*. Consequently, I have referenced consistently each grammar point to other relevant grammar points. As a result, you can explore The Workbook by using only your current needs as your starting point. In fact, you may learn more by following the natural connections in grammar rather than by working from start to finish through The Workbook. Furthermore, you will be able to create a more complete picture of the map of grammar by approaching the subject in this holistic way.

Where you should begin

Start with the *Initial Self-Assessment* to determine your current state of knowledge. Remember that this exercise is a form of self-measurement and not a test. A *Final Self-Assessment* is waiting at the end of The Workbook for you to measure how you have changed your knowledge. Use the results of your *Initial Self-Assessment* to establish on which parts of the book you should focus. Use the table of *Contents* to find your way around the book. Scan also the *Glossary* in the *Appendices* to find both the gaps in your knowledge and to consolidate your learning as you progress.

Initial self-assessment

Arrange the following words into the relevant boxes below.

writing	stapler	manager	spoken	would
gone	never	he	weight	think
keyboard	assistant	wrote	train	them
green	London	proofread	slowly	in
quietly	deliver	careful	see	went
happy	waited	mouse	answer	broken

Nouns

Adjectives

Verbs

Adverbs

Change the following into complete sentences where necessary.

In reply to your letter of 12 July regarding the change in the order of stock.

Introducing the new products onto the market with an eye to expanding throughout Europe.

Change the following sentences where necessary so that the subject and the verb agree.

The main role of the Team Managers are to co-ordinate the income-earning activities of the group.

None of these three proposals were accepted by the committee for inclusion in next year's budget.

Change the following sentences into the active voice where necessary.

Although the presentation was prepared weeks before the meeting, the overheads still had errors.

Martin reported the mistake to the Quality Team but nothing was done until it was too late.

Punctuate the following sentences where necessary.

the company which is based outside the city hopes to join the scheme in august they expect to see the difference which the benefits will make to their profits by the end of the year

nevertheless we have found four reasons to change the system the rising cost of production the shortage of adequately trained staff the low quality of our materials and the lack of sufficient storage space

Proofread and correct the following paragraph where necessary.

He summer sail is not on. All items will be hall-price form 4
July. No on can afford to miss his opportunity so get down to
the superstore to day

Initial self-assessment solution

Arrange the following words into the relevant boxes below.

writing	stapler	manager	spoken	would
gone	never	he	weight	think
keyboard	assistant	wrote	train	them
green	London	proofread	slowly	in
quietly	deliver	careful	see	went
happy	waited	mouse	answer	broken

Nouns

writing	green	London	mouse	answer
keyboard	stapler	manager	weight	them
	assistant	he	train	

Adjectives

gone	green	proofread	spoken	broken
	happy	careful	in	

Verbs

writing	deliver	proofread	see	think
gone	waited	spoken	answer	went
green	wrote	train	would	broken

Adverbs

quietly	never	slowly

Change the following into complete sentences where necessary.

I (subject) *reply* (main verb) to your letter of 12 July regarding the change in the order of stock.

_____

We (subject) *are introducing* (main verb) the new products onto the market with an eye to expanding throughout Europe.

Change the following sentences where necessary so that the subject and the verb agree.

The main *role* (subject) of the Team Managers *is* (main verb) to co-ordinate the income-earning activities of the group.

_____

None (subject) of these three proposals *was* (main verb) accepted by the committee for inclusion in next year's budget.

Change the following sentences into the active voice where necessary.

Although *someone* (subject) *had prepared* (main verb) the presentation weeks before the meeting, the overheads still had errors.

_____

Martin (subject) *reported* (main verb) the mistake to the Quality Team but *no one* (subject) *did* (main verb) *anything* (object) until *it* (subject) *was* (main verb) too late.

Punctuate the following sentences where necessary.

(T)he company(,) which is based outside the city(,) hopes to join the scheme in (A)ugust(.) (T)hey expect to see the difference which the benefits will make to their profits by the end of the year(.)

(N)evertheless(,) we have found four reasons to change the system(:) the rising cost of production(;) the shortage of adequately(-)trained staff(;) the low quality of our materials(;) and the lack of sufficient storage space(.)

Proofread and correct the following paragraph where necessary.

(T)he summer sa(le) is no(w) on. All items will be hal(f)-price f(ro)m 4 July. No on(e) can afford to miss (t)his opportunity so get down to the superstore to()day(.)

PART ONE

The parts of speech

1.1 **Preview**

The types of words and their function

We are going to look firstly at the *types* of words which we use and their *function*. We will look at words in terms of two broad groups. These two groups tell us the two main distinctions which we make in order to write about the world. Furthermore, we will look at open and closed classes of words within these two broad groups. We can create new words in the open classes but the closed classes are fixed.

The noun group of words

We will look firstly at distinguishing *objects* in the world. Consequently, we will look at the noun group of words. The words which I have included in the noun group are nouns; pronouns; adjectives; prepositions; and articles and determiners. Pronouns are by definition a type of noun; however, we will look at pronouns in their own section because pronouns are relatively complicated.

The verb group of words

We will look secondly at distinguishing *actions* in the world. Consequently, we will look at the verb group of words. I have included only verbs and adverbs in the verb group of words. I have chosen to write about verb conjugation and tense in Section Two where we will look at *groups of words*. I have related verb conjugation and tense to forming sentences.

Numerals and conjunctions

We will look also at how we use numerals in writing since a large part of business writing involves writing about *numbers*. Finally, we will look at conjunctions because conjunctions will provide us with a link into exploring sentences. However, we will look at sentences in detail in Part Two only.

The place of interjections

I have chosen to avoid looking in detail at interjections in The Workbook. I feel that interjections have little place in business writing even though interjections are a part of speech. However, I have made some references to interjections throughout The Workbook. You will find these references mostly under Exclamation Marks in Punctuation which is in Part Three.

1.2 **Nouns**

The function of nouns
We use nouns to identify *objects*. We also call nouns *naming words* because nouns are the names we give to things to distinguish those things from other things. Nouns are usually the words which we learn firstly when we learn a language. We have a number of types of nouns in English.

The types of nouns

Common nouns
We use common nouns to name *ordinary objects* such as *books* or *meetings*. We always write common nouns with a small or lower case letter unless the common noun starts a sentence (see also Punctuation). We always start a sentence with a capital or upper case letter.

Proper nouns
We use proper nouns to give an *official name* to an object on top of that object's common noun name. We use proper nouns to name specific people, cities, countries, places, and organisations such as *Shakespeare*, *Toronto*, *Peru*, *The Himalayas*, and *The New York Stock Exchange*.

We always write proper nouns with a capital or upper case letter no matter where we put the proper noun in the sentence (see also Punctuation).

Pronouns
We use pronouns as a *substitute* for nouns. In other words, we use pronouns such as *he*, *she*, or *it* to avoid repeating the noun. We will explore pronouns in more detail in their own section since we have a number of types of pronouns in English (see Pronouns).

Collective nouns
We use collective nouns to name groups of people or objects such as *team* or *department*. Collective nouns are always *singular* even though collective nouns name something made up of more than one thing (see also Subject and Verb Agreement).

Countable nouns
We use countable nouns to name things which we can count such as *four* **tables** or *one* **machine**. Consequently, we can form countable nouns into plurals. We use the adjective *few* to write about quantity

with countable nouns (see also Adjectives). We write that *we hope to make **fewer** mistakes in future*. We use adjectives to *describe* objects.

Uncountable nouns

We use uncountable nouns to name the things which we cannot count such as *weather* or *air*. Consequently, we cannot form uncountable nouns into plurals so uncountable nouns are always *singular* (see also Subject and Verb Agreement). We use the adjective *less* to write about quantity with uncountable nouns (see also Adjectives). We write that *we have **less** money now*.

Abstract nouns

We use abstract nouns to name things which are not concrete. In other words, we use abstract nouns to identify the things which we can experience but not touch. We use abstract nouns to name emotions such as *anger*; values such as *charity*; concepts such as *progress*; and principles such as *justice*.

We can use abstract nouns as either common nouns or proper nouns. Consequently, we can write abstract nouns with either a lower case or an upper case letter depending on how we use the word. Abstract nouns are always uncountable nouns. Consequently, we can never *quantify* abstract nouns although we can *measure* some of the things which we are naming.

Gerunds

We use gerunds to name *concepts* which we derive from *actions*. In other words, gerunds are the names which we give to the nouns which we have formed from verbs. Verbs are words which we use to identify actions. Typical examples of gerunds from business language are the *buy**ing***, the *sell**ing***, the *lower**ing***, the *cost**ing***, and the *budget**ing***.

We form gerunds with the present participle which is the *–ing* suffix or ending. Consequently, we can confuse the gerund easily with a continuous tense verb (see also Verbs and Tense). However, we form the continuous tense with the auxiliary verb *to be* such as ***are** buying* and ***is** selling*. An auxiliary verb is a verb which helps the main verb.

Notice that we can put an article such as *a*, *an*, or *the* in front of the gerund as we can with all nouns (see also Articles). The presence of an article such as *the* or the auxiliary verb *to be* will help us to distinguish gerunds from continuous tense verbs.

Subject nouns and object nouns

We can have a number of nouns in one sentence and so we need to distinguish between these nouns. However, we distinguish these nouns according to their *function* rather than according to their *type*.

Nouns have a relationship with the main or finite verb of a sentence.

The main or finite verb is the word which indicates both an *action* and a *tense* (see also Verbs). Some nouns *perform* the action of the main verb. We call these nouns the *subject* of the sentence. Other nouns *receive* the action of the main verb. We call these nouns the *object* of the sentence (see also Sentences).
Roberta (subject) *called* (main verb) *the client* (object).

Word building   We use word building to create new words in English. We build new words by adding prefixes and suffixes to root words. We add prefixes to the *beginning* of root words and we add suffixes to the *end* of root words.
Un- (prefix) *plus* **comfort** (root word) *plus* **-able** (suffix) *equals* **uncomfortable**.

Sometimes we join two root words to create new words. We often use root words from other languages to create new English words. In particular, we often use words from Greek and Latin.

Bio- from Greek meaning **life** *plus* **-logy** *from Greek meaning* **study** *equals* **biology** *in English meaning* **the study of life**.

Word building illustrates the dynamic and synthetic nature of semantics or *meaning* in English. Word building also illustrates the variety of influences in English which accounts for our extensive vocabulary.

Short cut grammar tips for nouns   We can test a noun by putting an article such as *a, an, or the* in front of the word.
A book; *an envelope*; or *the pen* (see also Articles).

Sometimes we use the same word both as a verb and as a noun (see also Verbs). Consequently, we need to focus on how words *function* in sentences rather than on what words *mean*.
I am going on **a walk** (noun).
I am going **to walk** (verb).

We can identify a gerund by looking to see whether or not the auxiliary verb *to be* precedes the word (see also Verbs).
The (article) **lowering** (gerund) *of costs is the priority of the team.*
The department manager **is** (auxiliary verb *to be*) **lowering** (continuous tense verb) *the cost of production.*

We can create new nouns, verbs, adjectives, and adverbs with word building (see also Verbs, Adjectives, and Adverbs). In other words, we can create new words in the four open classes of words. We use verbs to *identify actions*; we use adjectives to *describe objects*; and we use adverbs to *describe actions*. Sometimes, we use word building merely to change a root word from one open class to another.

Nominalisation

We use nominalisation to turn a verb into a noun. We turn verbs into nouns through the technique of word building (see also Word Building opposite). We use verbs to identify *actions* and so nominalisation is the process of turning an *action* into a *concept*. We have seen nominalisation already when we examined gerunds (see Gerunds).

We have a number of suffixes which we use to turn verbs into nouns. A suffix is a particle which we add to the *end* of a word to change the word's meaning. I have listed these suffixes below.

Verb	Suffix	Noun
to condemn	-tion	condemna**tion**
to measure	-ment	measure**ment**
to ally	-ance	alli**ance**
to suspend	-ense	susp**ense**
to expose	-ure	expos**ure**
to wreck	-age	wreck**age**

Writing tips for nouns

Using nominalisation will create a more formal style to your writing and so a more formal tone. In other words, your writing will be more *distant* if you use verbs as nouns (see Nominalisation above).
The meeting (gerund) *of clients is restricted to the rooms on the third floor.*

Using verbs as verbs will create a more action-centred style in your writing and so a more action-centred tone. In other words, your writing will be more *dynamic* if you use verbs as verbs (see also Verbs).
We expect consultants to meet (verb) *their clients only in the rooms on the third floor.*

Noun exercises

Essential exercise Circle the nouns below. Remember to test the word with an article to see if the word is a noun. Use *a*, *an*, or *the* in front of the word.

staff	sue	yours	drive	were
I	their	bad	feel	cord
send	file	see	loss	cut
speed	eat	long	could	extend
fast	find	it	you	serve
coach	end	now	goods	post
her	never	talks	red	drag
yet	shares	might	his	plain

Bridging exercise Circle the nouns below. Remember to test the word with an article to see if the word is a noun. Use *a*, *an*, or *the* in front of the word.

in-tray	shortish	orange	success	urgent
smoking	fraudster	finish	water	anger
clever	consult	itself	wasn't	panic
programme	letter	growing	pressure	will be
hopeful	audit	over here	clearly	return
badly	Europe	beauty	unique	defence
order	despair	denote	client	complaint
myself	slower	seldom	put aside	wanting

Applied exercise Circle the nouns below. Remember to test the word with an article to see if the word is a noun. Use *a*, *an*, or *the* in front of the word.

typically	Wall Street	beautiful	company	judgmental
Australia	manager	Japanese	relocate	consultant
sensitive	denotation	enclosure	selected	eraser
flawlessly	United Kingdom	anyway	operations	happier
salary	uncomfortable	advisor	breakfast	communicate
paper clip	Americanese	employer	necessary	inadvertently
secretary	hopelessly	FTSE 100	stupidly	capable
director	conglomerate	adamantly	projection	international

(For answers see pages 170–171)

1.3 **Pronouns**

The function of pronouns
We use pronouns as a *substitute* for nouns. In other words, we use pronouns such as *he*, *she*, or *it* to avoid repeating the noun. Nouns are words which we use to *identify* objects (see also Nouns). We can use pronouns to write about both people and things.

The types of pronouns
We have several types of pronouns in English. We will look firstly at the personal pronouns: *subject*; *object*; *possessive*; *genitive*; and *reflexive*. You will be able to test your knowledge of these pronouns with the essential and applied exercises below. Then we will look separately at *relative* and *interrogative* pronouns.

The personal pronouns

Subject pronouns
We use subject pronouns when the noun which we are replacing is the subject of the sentence. The subject of the sentence is the noun which *performs the action* of the main verb of the sentence (see also Sentences). A verb is a word which we use to *identify* an action. We use tense to indicate *when* we perform an action. A main verb is a word which we use to identify both an *action* and a *tense* (see also Verbs and Tense).

The singular subject pronouns are *I, you, he, she*, and *it*. The plural subject pronouns are *we, you*, and *they*.
I (subject) *am holding* (main verb) *the meeting* (object) *on Tuesday*.

Object pronouns
We use object pronouns when the noun which we are replacing is the object of the sentence. The object of the sentence is the noun which *receives the action* of the main verb of the sentence (see also Sentences). A verb is a word which we use to *identify* an action. We use tense to indicate *when* we perform an action. A main verb is a word which we use to identify both an *action* and a *tense* (see also Verbs and Tense).

The singular object pronouns are *me, you, him, her*, and *it*. The plural object pronouns are *us, you*, and *them*.
Linda (subject) *drove* (main verb) **him** (object) *to the airport last week*.

Writing tips for pronouns

Avoid confusing the subject pronoun *I* with the object pronoun *me* in compound subjects and compound objects (see also Sentences).
We write *Harold and I went to the meeting* because we write *I went to the meeting*.
Moreover, we write *Pamela met **Harold and me** in the reception* because we write *Pamela met **me** in the reception* (see also Subject and Verb Agreement).

Avoid using the reflexive pronoun in the place of the object pronoun (see also Reflexive Pronouns).
Write *I have sent this to **yourselves*** as *I have sent this to **you***.

Avoid using the reflexive pronoun for *emphasis*. An emphatic tone implies that the user understands the context of the situation. Instead, *articulate* clearly the point of your statement.
*The consultant had to do the work **herself*** (emphatic tone).
The consultant had to do the work and so we wasted time which we could have used more productively (articulate tone).

Possessive pronouns

We use possessive pronouns when we want to show that something *belongs* to someone or something else. Some grammarians call possessive pronouns *possessive adjectives* (see also Adjectives).

The singular possessive pronouns are *my*, *your*, *his*, *her*, and *its*. The plural possessive pronouns are *our*, *your*, and *their*.
*Barry put the laptop in **my** office overnight.*

Notice that the possessive pronoun *its* takes no apostrophe even though the word indicates possession (see also Punctuation).

Genitive pronouns

We use genitive pronouns for two reasons. Firstly, we use genitive pronouns when we want to show that something *belongs* to someone or something else.

Secondly, we use genitive pronouns when we use a pronoun as a predicative adjective (see also Adjectives). In this case, the genitive pronoun follows the verb *to be* which is an intransitive verb (see also Verbs). We call a verb *intransitive* when the verb cannot take an object. An object is a noun which *receives the action* of the main verb of a sentence (see also Sentences). A main verb is a word which we use to identify both an *action* and a *tense* (see also Tense). We use tense to indicate *when* we perform an action.
*The car is **hers**.*

The singular genitive pronouns are *mine*, *yours*, *his*, *hers* and *its*. The plural genitive pronouns are *ours*, *yours* and *theirs*.

Reflexive
pronouns

We use reflexive pronouns for two reasons. Firstly, we use reflexive pronouns when the subject of the sentence performs an action on itself. In other words, the subject *reflects* the action of the main verb back to the subject (see also Sentences).

I (subject) gave (main verb) **myself** *an hour to finish the report.*

Secondly, we use reflexive pronouns for *emphasis*. In other words, we can use the reflexive pronoun emphatically. The emphatic use of the reflexive pronoun is typical of spoken English and will create a conversational or emphatic tone in our writing (see also Style and Tone). *The consultant had to do the work* **herself** *(because no one else was available).*

The singular reflexive pronouns are *myself, yourself, himself, herself,* and *itself.* The plural reflexive pronouns are *ourselves, yourselves,* and *themselves.*

Personal pronouns exercises

Essential exercise

Write the correct personal pronoun into the following sentences.

First person singular *I* own the book. The book belongs to ___. No one may take ___ book. The book is _____. I bought the book for _____.	**Second person singular** *You* own the book. The book belongs to ____. No one may take _____ book. The book is _____. You bought the book for _____.
Third person singular masculine *He* owns the book. The book belongs to ____. No one may take ____ book. The book is ____. He bought the book for _____.	**Third person singular feminine** *She* owns the book. The book belongs to ____. No one may take ____ book. The book is _____. She bought the book for _____.
Third person singular neutral *It* owns the book. The book belongs to ___. No one may take ____ book. The book is ____. It bought the book for _____.	**First person plural** *We* own the book. The book belongs to ___. No one may take ____ book. The book is _____. We bought the book for _____.

Second person plural	**Third person plural**
You own the book.	*They* own the book.
The book belongs to ____.	The book belongs to _____.
No one may take _____ book.	No one may take _____ book.
The book is _____.	The book is _____.
You bought the book for	They bought the book for
_____.	_____.

Applied exercise   Complete the following table of personal pronouns.

Person	**Subject pronoun**	**Object pronoun**	**Possessive pronoun**	**Genitive pronoun**	**Reflexive pronoun**
First Person Singular:	I			mine	
Second Person Singular:			your		yourself
Third Person Singular (Masculine):		him			
Third Person Singular (Feminine):	she				
Third Person Singular (Neutral):			its		itself
First Person Plural:				ours	
Second Person Plural:		you			
Third Person Plural:	they				

(For answers see pages 172–173)

Other types of pronouns

Relative
pronouns

We use relative pronouns to add extra information to sentences. Relative pronouns introduce relative clauses. Clauses are groups of words which contain a main verb but which are not independent sentences (see also Phrases and Clauses). A verb is a word which we use to *identify* an action. A main verb is a word which we use to identify both an *action* and a *tense* (see also Verbs, Sentences, and Tense). Relative clauses can be defining and non-defining.

Defining relative
clauses

We use defining relative clauses to provide extra information which *defines* or *identifies* the subject or the object of a sentence. In other words, the identity of the subject or the object of the sentence is *dependent* on the extra information (see also Sentences). Consequently, we also call defining relative clauses *identifying relative clauses* (see also Phrases and Clauses). We never use a comma before or after defining relative clauses (see also Punctuation). *The courier* **who arrived late** (defining relative clause) *delivered our package to reception.*

Non-defining
relative clauses

We use non-defining relative clauses to provide extra information about an already defined or identified subject or object of a sentence. In other words, the identity the subject or the object of the sentence is *independent* of the extra information (see also Sentences). Consequently, we also call non-defining relative clauses *non-identifying relative clauses* (see also Phrases and Clauses). We always use a comma *before and after* a non-defining relative clause (see also Punctuation).
Henry, **who is always late,** (non-defining relative clause) *has been appointed to the committee.*

The types of relative pronouns

We have five relative pronouns: *who, whom, whose, that,* and *which.*

Who and whom

Who is the subject relative pronoun and we use **who** to add *extra information* to a sentence about the subject of that sentence (see also Sentences). We use the relative pronoun **who** for people only.
The person **who** *took the stationery without permission must return everything immediately.*

Whom is the object relative pronoun and we use **whom** to add *extra information* to a sentence about the object of that sentence (see also Sentences). We use the relative pronoun **whom** for people only.
The person to **whom** *I originally spoke has left the company.*

We also can use the relative pronoun *that* instead of **who** or **whom** for people. However, we *reify* people when we use the relative pronoun *that* instead of **who** or **whom**. We say that we have *reified* someone when we turn that person into an object (see also Style and Tone).
*The person **that** took the stationery without permission must return everything immediately.*
*The person **that** I originally spoke to has left the company.*

Whose

Whose is the possessive relative pronoun and we use **whose** to show *possession* in the extra information which we are adding to a sentence. We use **whose** for all things including people, animals, and objects.
*We will reprimand the person **whose** laptop was left overnight in the office.*
*We took the chair **whose** leg someone had broken.*

That and which

We use *that* to add *extra information* to a sentence about objects, animals, and people.
*We will reward the team **that** achieves the highest targets.*

We also can use *that* after a speech verb in indirect speech although using *that* is not always necessary (see also Direct and Indirect Speech). Using *that* after a speech verb will make our writing more formal in tone (see also Style and Tone). Omitting *that* will make our writing more conversational in tone.
*Frances said **that** she could not attend the away-day.*
Frances said she could not attend the away-day

We use **which** to add *extra information* to a sentence about objects and animals only. We use **who** and **whom** for people.
*The disk **which** was on the table is gone.*

We can use *that* and **which** interchangeably in some cases. We create a more formal tone in our writing when we use **which**. Equally, we create a more conversational tone in our writing when we use *that* (see also Style and Tone).
*The department **which** achieves the highest results will be rewarded (formal tone).*
*The department **that** achieves the highest results will be rewarded (conversational tone).*

Interrogative pronouns

The function of interrogative pronouns

We use interrogative pronouns to ask open questions. The adjective *interrogative* comes from the verb *to interrogate* which means *to ask questions*. Open questions are particularly useful for gathering information, mentoring, coaching, and counselling (see also Verbs for Auxiliary Verbs and Closed Questions). Open questions always end in a question mark like all questions (see also Punctuation).

The types of interrogative pronouns

We have seven interrogative pronouns: *who, what, which, when, where, why,* and *how*.

We use **who** for people.
Who *decided to buy this product?*

We use **what** and **which** for animals, objects, and the unknown. We also use **what** for *open* questions and **which** for *specific* questions.
What *type of dogs do you breed?* Or **which** *type of dogs do you breed?*
What *computer do you use?* Or **which** *computer do you use?*
What *did you find?*

We use **when** for time.
When *did you arrive?* (See also Adverbs of Time)

We use **where** for place.
Where *did you go?* (See also Adverbs of Place)

We use **how** for manner.
How *did you do the survey?* (See also Adverbs of Manner)

We use **why** for reason.
Why *did you say what you said?*

Writing tips for relative pronouns

Use the relative pronoun *who* for people. We reify people when we use the relative pronoun *that* for a person. We say that we have reified someone when we have turned that person into an object.
*We asked the man **that** arrived late to wait* (reified).
*We asked the man **who** arrived late to wait* (personified).

Use the relative pronoun *which* to make your writing *more* formal. Use the relative pronoun *that* to make your writing *less* formal.
*We will reward the team **which** comes first* (more formal).
*We will reward the team **that** comes first* (less formal).

Use the object relative pronoun *whom* to make your writing *more* formal. Furthermore, you can avoid ending a sentence with a preposition if you use the object relative pronoun *whom* (see also Prepositions). Use the subject relative pronoun *who* for the object of the sentence to make your writing *more* conversational.
*Can you tell me **to whom** I should sent the package?* (Formal)
*Can you tell me **who** I should sent the package **to**?* (Conversational)

1.4 **Adjectives**

The function and types of adjectives

We use adjectives to *describe* nouns so adjectives give us more information about *objects*. Adjectives can tell us about colour: *the **green** car*. Adjectives can tell us about size: *a **big** room*. Adjectives can tell us about shape: *the **round** table*. Furthermore, adjectives can tell us about weight: *a **heavy** engine*.

We have five specific types of adjectives other than the general adjectives which I have described in the paragraph above.

Demonstrative adjectives

We use demonstrative adjectives to indicate three things. Firstly, demonstrative adjectives tell us about *which* object we are writing. Secondly, demonstrative adjectives tell us how *near* or *far* that object is in both space and time. Finally, demonstrative adjectives tell us whether that object is *singular* or *plural*. Some grammarians classify demonstrative adjectives as *determiners* (see also Articles and Determiners).
***This** chair over here* and ***that** chair over there.*
***These** chairs over here* and ***those** chairs over there.*

Comparative adjectives

We can use adjectives to compare the *qualities* of one thing to the *qualities* of another. We call these adjectives *comparative adjectives*. We use the structure *as* (adjective) *as* to make comparisons. We also use the structure (adjective) *-er than* to make comparisons with words of one or two syllables. Finally, we use the structure *more* (adjective) *than* to make comparisons with words of two or more syllables.
***As** big* (adjective) ***as** a house* and ***as** tall* (adjective) ***as** a tree.*
*He is **faster** (adjective) **than** I (am fast).*

Superlative adjectives

We can use adjectives to explain that the *qualities* of one thing are the best out of the *qualities* of three or more things. We call these adjectives *superlative adjectives*. We use the structure *the* (adjective) *–est* to form superlatives out of words of one or two syllables. We also use the structure *the most* (adjective) to form superlatives out of words of two or more syllables.
*The first machine is **the slowest** (adjective) of the five machines.*
*She is **the most** intelligent (adjective) member of the team.*

Compound adjectives	We form compound adjectives by joining two or more independent words to form one concept. Consequently, we always hyphenate compound adjectives (see also Punctuation). *The **three-day** event* and *a **button-down** shirt*.

We always hyphenate some prefixes when these prefixes form part of compound adjectives. Prefixes are particles or parts of words which we put *in front* of a root word to change the root word's *meaning* or *function* (see also Word Building below). We also use short words as prefixes. Prefixes which we always hyphenate include *well-*, *self-*, *non-*, and *ex-*.
***Well-**formed*, ***self-**aware*, ***non-**specific* and ***ex-**partner*.

We also use adverbs to form compound adjectives. Adverbs are words which we use to *describe actions* (see also Adverbs). Adverbs usually *end* in the suffix *–ly*. A suffix is a particle or a part of a word which we put at the *end* of a root word to change the root word's *meaning* or *function* (see also Word Building below). We always hyphenate adverbs when we use adverbs in compound adjectives (see also Puctuation).
*A **highly-defined** concept* and *a **rapidly-developing** market*.

Possessive adjectives	We use possessive adjectives to indicate that an object *belongs* to someone or something else. Consequently, we say that possessive adjectives indicate *possession*. Some grammarians classify possessive adjectives as *possessive pronouns* (see also Pronouns). Notice that the possessive adjective *its* takes no apostrophe even though the word indicates possession. We use apostrophes to indicate possession and contraction (see also Punctuation). ***My** team* and ***their** work*.

Predicative adjectives	Sometimes we use the predicate of a sentence as an adjective. The predicate of a sentence is everything in the sentence other than the subject. The subject of a sentence is the noun which *performs* the action of the main verb. The main verb is the word which tells us an *action* and a *tense*. Consequently, the predicate of a sentence includes the main verb (see also Sentences).

We can write *the **courageous** man* as *the man* (subject) *is **courageous*** (predicate). Furthermore, we can write *the **hard-working** woman* as *the woman* (subject) *is **hard-working*** (predicate).

Predicative adjectives always follow the verb *to be* which is an intransitive verb. Intransitive verbs cannot take an object (see also Verbs). The object of a sentence is the noun which *receives* the action of the main verb (see also Sentences). Other examples of intransitive verbs are the verbs *to seem* and *to appear*.

Word building
We use word building to create new words in English. We build new words by adding prefixes and suffixes to root words. We add prefixes to the *beginning* of root words and we add suffixes to the *end* of root words.

Un- (prefix) *plus* **comfort** (root word) *plus* **-able** (suffix) *equals* **uncomfortable**.

We can create new nouns, verbs, adjectives, and adverbs with word building (see also Nouns, Verbs and Adverbs). In other words, we can create new words in the four open classes of words. We use nouns to *identify objects*; we use verbs to *identify actions*; and we use adverbs to *describe actions*. Sometimes we use word building merely to change a root word from one open class to another.

We always use certain suffixes to form root words into adjectives. I have listed below the suffixes which we use to form root words into adjectives.

Root word	Suffix	Adjective
to afford	-able	afford**able**
to determine	-ed	determin**ed**
the nation	-al	nation**al**
long	-ish	long**ish**
fast	-est	the fast**est**
big	-er	bigg**er**

Short cut grammar tips for adjectives
Test a word to see if the word is an adjective by putting the word in the position of the predicate of the sentence (see also Sentences).
*The **blue** form* becomes *the form is **blue**.*
*The **hardworking** team* becomes *the team is **hardworking**.*

Writing tips for adjectives
Consider carefully the number of adjectives which you use in business writing. Sometimes we can obscure the subject of the sentence with too many adjectives. Remember the guideline of limiting your sentences to one or two *ideas* (see also Sentences).

Use only the adjectives which give the user *essential information* about the subject. Ask yourself what the user needs to know so that he or she can *understand* and *accept* your message.

Adjective exercises

Circle the adjectives below. Remember to test the word to see if it is an adjective by putting the word in front of a noun. Remember also to test the word by putting the word in the position of the predicate of the sentence. Use a form such as "the object is (word)".

you	start	short	down	it's
would	book	me	dial	lunch
long	that	type	do	print
ours	sue	chair	yours	his
still	staple	switch	there	should
meet	pay	this	phone	your
slow	clean	freeze	fast	doubt
plan	hope	weak	bound	press

Bridging exercise   Circle the adjectives below. Remember to test the word to see if it is an adjective by putting the word in front of a noun. Remember also to test the word by putting the word in the position of the predicate of the sentence. Use a form such as "the object is (word)".

copy	friendly	ugly	over there	anxious
themselves	smaller	dinner	author	weren't
faster	stapler	eager	habit	hopeful
enclose	rising	frowning	customs	crushing
yellow	save in	major	denial	icy
contact	suspend	slowly	urgent	neatly
England	laptop	herself	issues	won't
failure	spiral	button	confirm	declare

Applied exercise   Circle the adjectives below. Remember to test the word to see if it is an adjective by putting the word in front of a noun. Remember also to test the word by putting the word in the position of the predicate of the sentence. Use a form such as "the object is (word)".

unavoidably	commencement	inexpressibly	immediate	receptionist
suspension	management	division	cleverly	fraudulent
computer	establish	substantial	Canada	West Indies
touchy-feely	interpersonal	stationary	reception	immediately
establishment	connotation	terminate	engineer	European
police officer	associate	mistakenly	nevertheless	multinational
prejudiced	New Zealand	redundancy	purchasing	erroneous
corroborate	reify	well-illustrated	remunerate	exemplify

(For answers see pages 174–175)

1.5 **Articles and determiners**

The function and type of articles

We use articles to provide more information about nouns. Nouns are words which we use to *identify objects* (see also Nouns). Consequently, articles are similar in *function* to adjectives (see also Adjectives).

We have only three articles in English. We have two indefinite articles and one definite article.

The indefinite articles

We use the indefinite articles to refer to nouns which are *unspecified*. The two indefinite articles are **a** and **an**.

We use the indefinite article **a** in front of nouns which begin with consonants. Consonants are the twenty-one letters of the English alphabet which are not vowels. The five vowels are *a, e, i, o,* and *u*.
A pen or *a computer*.

We use the indefinite article **an** in front of nouns which begin with one of the five vowels. The five vowels are *a, e, i, o,* and *u*.
An envelope or *an office*.

Indefinite articles and adjectives

Adjectives are words which we use to describe nouns and we put adjectives between the article and the noun. A noun is a word which we use to *identify objects*. The first letter of the adjective will determine which indefinite article we use in front of the adjective.
An underrated worker or *a torn envelope*.

Exceptions with indefinite articles and adjectives

We have some exceptions to the rules for articles in English. We use the indefinite article **a** when the first letter of a word is a vowel but *sounds* like a consonant. Similarly, we use the indefinite article **an** when the first letter of a word is a consonant but *sounds* like a vowel. The *sound* of the letter will then determine which indefinite article we use in front of the noun or the adjective. Say the word to yourself to hear the difference. The five vowels are *a, e, i, o,* and *u*. Consonants are the twenty-one letters of the English alphabet which are not vowels.
A university degree and *an hour of someone's time*.
An umbrella and *a hotel*.

The definite article

We use the definite article *the* to refer to *specific people or things*. We have only one definite article in English. We use the definite article *the* in front of words which begin with both consonants and vowels. *The* keyboard or *the* driver.

The function of determiners

We use determiners in a similar way to articles and like articles, determiners *function* also as adjectives (see also Adjectives). Determiners tell us three things. Firstly, determiners tell us to *which* object we are referring. Secondly, determiners tell us whether that object is *near or far away in either time or space*. Lastly, determiners tell us whether the object is *singular* or *plural*.
This book or **that** *pile of paper.*
These books or **those** *piles of paper.*

Writing tips for articles and determiners

We use the object pronoun *them* instead of the determiner *those* in some forms of spoken English. We say *hand me* **them** *books.* A plural determiner would be more appropriate since we use Standard English in business writing. Write instead *hand me* **those** *books.*

1.6 **Prepositions**

The function of prepositions We use prepositions to indicate *position* and *movement*. The *function* of prepositions is easier to remember when we notice that the word *preposition* contains the word *position*.

The types of prepositions

Prepositions of position We use prepositions of *position* to indicate where people, animals, and objects are placed. Prepositions of position usually follow the verb *to be* which identifies the *state* of people, animals, and objects. The verb *to be* is an intransitive verb which means that the verb cannot take an object (see also Verbs). The object of a sentence is the noun which receives the action of the main verb of the sentence (see also Sentences).

The verb *to be* also introduces a predicative adjective (see also Adjectives and Phrases and Clauses). Consequently, prepositions of *position* often introduce an adjectival phrase. In other words, the group of words which follows the preposition *describes* the noun. A noun is a word which we use to *identify an object* (see also Nouns). *The mistake* (noun) *was* (main verb *to be* – past tense) **in** *the system*. *The consultants* (noun) *are* (main verb *to be* – present tense) **out** *with clients*.

Prepositions of position include: *in, inside, out, outside, above, below, next to, between, in front, behind, together,* and *under*.

Prepositions of movement We use prepositions of *movement* to indicate how or where people, animals, and objects are moving. These prepositions usually follow a main verb of movement such as *to go* or *to walk*. We can use main verbs of movement intransitively which means that we can follow these verbs with a predicative adjective (see also Verbs and Adjectives). However, prepositions of movement usually follow a verb which identifies an action as opposed to a state of existence. Consequently, prepositions of movement often introduce an adverbial phrase (see also Phrases and Clauses). In other words, the group of words which follows the preposition tells us more information about the verb (see also Adverbs).

*Move the boxes **to** the other side of the room.*
*Go **to** reception and ask **for** the key.*

Prepositions of movement include: *to, for, in, inside, out, outside, under, over, next to, between, through, in front, behind,* and *across.* Many of the prepositions of movement are the same as the prepositions of position. However, the *meaning* of these prepositions differs according to how the preposition *functions* in the sentence.

Prepositions and phrasal verbs

Sometimes prepositions form part of a verb phrase. We call these verbs *phrasal verbs.* A phrasal verb consists of a main verb and a preposition. A main verb is a word which identifies an *action* and a *tense* (see also Verbs). The preposition is essential to the meaning of the verb. Consequently, we see the verb and the preposition as one thing and so together the verb and the preposition form a phrase.

Writing tips for prepositions

Some people think that finishing a sentence with a preposition is incorrect. However, perhaps we could describe this style more accurately as being typical of spoken English. Avoid finishing your sentences with a preposition if you chose to use a formal style in your writing.
What did you put the papers in? (Informal style)
In what did you put the papers? (Formal style)

Write as you speak if you choose to use an informal or conversational style in your writing. In other words, finishing your sentences with a preposition would create a relaxed and informal style. Establish your purpose clearly before you start writing and then allow your style to follow from the guiding principle of your purpose.
To whom did you speak? (Formal style)
Who did you speak to? (Informal or conversational style)
(See also Relative Pronouns for the last example)

Some people consider the use of phrasal verbs to be a symptom of a lazy writing style. However, perhaps we could better describe phrasal verbs as *emphatic.* In other words, we use phrasal verbs for *emphasis.* Phrasal verbs tend to be characteristic of spoken English and so we can use phrasal verbs to create an informal style in our writing.

Consider carefully the context of your writing. Use a main verb alone if the *meaning* of the action is clear. In other words, use a phrasal verb only if the preposition will *clarify* the meaning of the main verb. For example, *report* and *report back* mean the same thing as do *join* and *join together.* However, *stand* could mean *stand up* or *stand out* and *sit* could mean *sit down* or *sit up* (see also Style and Tone).

However, we can separate the main verb and the preposition with additional information (see also Style and Tone).
*We have finally **settled in** after four months.*
*The department **sent** the leaflets **out** and is waiting for a response.*

Prepositions across languages

People who work with people from other cultures and with other languages need to be aware of some of the difficulties around prepositions. Prepositions are usually the last words which we learn when we learn another language. Prepositions are difficult to learn because their meaning is usually *conventional*. In other words, we accept the meaning of prepositions through agreement. Consequently, prepositions are difficult to translate across languages. For example, in Italian we write *I am going in London* and not *I am going to London*. Translating *directly* from one language to another can lead to misunderstanding in business writing.

Preposition exercises

Essential exercise

Complete the following word combinations by adding a preposition.

thanks ___	apart _____	further ___
save ___	instead ___	owing ___
short ___	along_____	outside___
down ___	away _____	prior ___
due ___	because ___	except ____
care ___	subject ___	as well ___

Bridging exercise

Complete the following word combinations by adding a preposition.

by means ___	in case ___	relative ___
by way ___	in terms ___	as opposed ___
in lieu ___	according ___	in contrast _____
in line _____	contrary ___	in contrast ___
in spite ___	together _____	in favour ___
on top ___	regardless ___	in keeping _____

Applied exercise   Complete the following word combinations by adding a preposition.

accompanied ___   on behalf ___   in the case ___

irrespective ___   with respect ___   in the course ___

subsequent ___   with regard ___   in the line ___

in regard ___   in addition ___   on the grounds ___

in respect ___   in common _____   in conjunction _____

in response ___   with reference ___   in connection _____

in return ____   as a result ___   in accordance _____

on account ___   on the part ___   in comparison _____

(For answers see page 176)

1.7 **Verbs**

The function of verbs

We use verbs to *identify actions*. We also call verbs *doing words* because verbs indicate what people, animals, and things are doing. We also use verbs to *identify states of being*. Verbs are usually the words which we learn after nouns when we are learning a language. We have several types of verbs in English.

The types of verbs

Infinitive verbs

We use infinitive verbs to write about actions or states as concepts such as *to speak* or *to be*. We call these verbs *infinitives* because infinitives have no tense. We do not think of infinitives as happening at a specific time. Instead, infinitives are without time. We can use more than one infinitive in a sentence.

Infinitives usually have the preposition *to* in front of the verb. However, infinitives after a modal verb never take the preposition *to* such as *can meet, might go,* or *would be* (see also Prepositions). A modal verb is a verb which *modifies* the main verb of a sentence (see also Verbs and Modals and Conditionals).

The split infinitive

We split the infinitive when we put an adverb between the preposition *to* and the verb such as *to quickly type*. Instead, we should write *to type quickly* or *quickly to type*.

In Latin, the infinitive verb is a single word. We took our formal grammar in English from Latin and so the pioneer grammarians considered the infinitive verb in English to be *one* word.

Traditionally, grammarians have thought that splitting the infinitive verb is wrong. However, many grammarians now consider the split infinitive as a mark of poor style rather than as a mark of poor grammar (see also Adverbs). We can also consider the split infinitive to be a mark of an emphatic or conversational style (see also Style and Tone).

Finite or main verbs

We use main verbs to identify *actions or states* but main verbs also identify the tense of the verb or *when the action or state happened*. The tense of the main verb will tell us whether the action took place in the *past*, the *present*, or the *future* (see also Tense).

The tense of the main verb will tell us also whether the action was in the *simple*, *continuous*, or *perfect* tense. We never use the preposition *to* in front of a main verb and we can have only one main verb in a sentence (see also Sentences).

However, we use a second main verb when we join two sentences with a conjunction or an adverb of time (see also Adverbs and Conjunctions). We use an adverb of time to tell us *when* the two main verbs happened in relation to each other (see also Adverbs).
Way Lin called (main verb – past simple) *the client **and*** (conjunction) *secured* (main verb – past simple) *the contract.*
Deirdre filed (main verb – past simple) *the complaint **before*** (adverb of time) *she notified* (main verb – past simple) *the committee.*

Transitive verbs Transitive verbs are main verbs which can take an object. The prefix *trans-* means *to cross*. In other words, someone or something can *receive* the action of the main verb (see also Sentences). We can *transfer the action* of the main verb to someone or something else. Consequently, we can form transitive verbs into passive verbs (see also Voice).
We (subject) ***planned*** (transitive main verb) *the meeting* (object).
The meeting (object) ***was planned*** (passive main verb) *by us* (subject).

Intransitive verbs Intransitive verbs are main verbs which cannot take an object. In other words, we have nothing concrete which can *receive* the action of the verb (see also Sentences). We cannot *transfer the action* to someone or something else. Consequently, we cannot form intransitive verbs into passive verbs (see also Voice).

However, we can use intransitive verbs to form predicative adjectives (see also Adjectives). The verbs *to be*, *to seem*, and *to appear* are all intransitive verbs. We also can use verbs such as *to go*, *to walk*, and *to ask* as intransitive verbs.
Rachel (subject) ***is*** (intransitive main verb) *calm* (adjective).
The team (subject) ***went*** (intransitive main verb) *to the conference* (prepositional phrase).

Auxiliary verbs We use auxiliary verbs to *help* the main verb of the sentence. We have only three auxiliary verbs in English which are *to be*, *to do*, and *to have*. Furthermore, we also can use all three auxiliary verbs as main verbs.

We use the auxiliary verb *to be* to form the continuous tense and the passive voice (see also Voice and Tense). We use the auxiliary verb *to do* to form negative statements. We use the auxiliary verb *to have* to form the perfect tense (see also Tense). Finally, we use all three auxiliary verbs to form closed questions.

*They **are delivering** the material* (continuous tense).
*The material **was delivered*** (passive voice).
*We **do not deliver** material* (negative statement).
*We **have delivered** the material* (perfect tense).
***Are we delivering** the material this time* (closed question)?
***Do we deliver** the material* (closed question)?
***Have we delivered** materials before* (closed question)?

Modal verbs

We use modal verbs to *modify* or change the main verb of the sentence. We use modal verbs to write about *possibility, certainty, permission,* and *intention*. The modal verbs are *may, might, can, could, will, would, shall, should, ought to,* and *have to*. We always follow modal verbs with an infinitive verb without the preposition *to* such as *could be* (see also Modals and Conditionals).

Passive verbs

We use passive verbs to create sentences which have no immediately identifiable subject (see also sentences). The subject of the sentence is the noun which performs the action of the main verb of the sentence (see also main verbs above).

Passive verbs allow us to do three things. Firstly, passive verbs allow us to write about an action when we do not know who was responsible for that action. Secondly, passive verbs allow us to emphasise the object of the sentence over the subject of the sentence when the object is more important. Finally, passive verbs allow us to hide the subject of the sentence.
My car (object) ***was stolen*** (passive main verb) *last night*.

We form passive verbs with the auxiliary verb *to be*; a main verb; and *one* of the past participles *-ed, -en,* or *–ne* (see also Active and Passive Voice). The auxiliary verb *to be* carries the tense of the verb (see also Tense).

Causative verbs

We use causative verbs to write about the actions which *we have caused someone else to perform for us*. Causative verbs are similar to passive verbs and so we often confuse the two verb types. However, causative verbs are not passive verbs simply because causative verbs identify an action which *we cannot do ourselves*. We use causative verbs when we want to indicate that the person who *caused* the action to happen is more important than the person who *performed* the action.

We form causative verbs with the auxiliary verb *to have*; a main verb; and *one* of the past participles *–ed, -en,* or *–ne*. The auxiliary verb *to have* carries the tense of the verb (see also Tense).
*Mark **had** his hair **cut*** (by a barber).

Copular verbs We use copular verbs to *join* the noun or adjective phrase to the subject of the sentence (see also Phrases and Clauses). We also call copular verbs *intransitive verbs* (see also Intransitive Verbs). We can test a verb to see if the verb is intransitive by turning the verb into a passive verb (see also Passive Verbs and Voice). We know that the verb is intransitive if we *cannot* change the verb into the passive voice.

Copular verbs include *be, get, become, seem, feel, appear, taste, look, sound,* and *smell.* These copular verbs usually introduce an adjective phrase which is a group of words which describes the noun (see also Adjectives and Phrases).

Copular verbs which introduce *change* include *get, turn, become, stay, grow, remain, go,* and *keep.* We can use *sit, stand, lie, fall, walk, go,* and *ask* also as copular verbs.

Contractions We use contractions in *spoken* English. We usually contract the verb to the subject of the sentence. We say *I'll* for *I will* and *can't* for *cannot.*

We show omission with an apostrophe whenever we omit letters in written English (see also Punctuation). Notice that *it's* means *it is.* We use no apostrophe for the possessive pronoun *its* (see also Pronouns). **It's** *raining* means **it is** *raining.* **Its** *cover* means the *cover belongs to it.*

Contractions are a choice of style in written English. Contractions make our writing seem more conversational or more informal (see also Style and Tone).

Compound verbs We often form verbs from more than one word. We call verbs made of more than one word *compound verbs.* We form compound verbs with the three auxiliary verbs *to be, to do,* and *to have* (see also Auxiliary Verbs). We use auxiliary verbs to *help* the main verb of the sentence.

The continuous tenses and the perfect tenses are all compound verbs (see also Tense). We also form the passive voice with a compound verb (see also Passive Verbs Voice).
We **are selling** (continuous tense) *our stock.*
We **have sold** (perfect tense) *our stock.*
Our stock **was sold** (passive verb).

Phrasal verbs and prepositions Sometimes we form verb phrases with prepositions. We call these verbs *phrasal verbs.* A phrasal verb consists of a main verb which is a verb with a tense and one or more prepositions. A preposition is a word which we use to indicate *position* and *movement* (see also

Prepositions). The preposition is essential to the meaning of the verb. Consequently, we see the verb and the preposition as one thing and so the verb and the preposition form a phrase (see also Verbs). However, we can separate the main verb and the preposition with additional information.

*We have finally **settled in** after four months.*

*The department **sent** the leaflets **out** and is waiting for a response.*

Word building

We use word building to create new words in English. We build new words by adding prefixes and suffixes to root words. We add prefixes to the *beginning* of root words and we add suffixes to the *end* of root words.

Un- (prefix) *plus* **comfort** (root word) *plus* **-able** (suffix) *equals* **uncomfortable**.

Sometimes we join root words to create new words. We often use root words from other languages to create new English words. In particular, we often use words from Greek and Latin.

Bio- *from Greek meaning* **life** *plus* **-logy** *from Greek meaning* **study** *equals* **biology** *in English meaning* **the study of life**.

Word building illustrates the dynamic and synthetic nature of semantics or *meaning* in English. Word building also illustrates the variety of influences in English which accounts for our extensive vocabulary.

We can create new nouns, verbs, adjectives, and adverbs with word building (see also Nouns, Adjectives, and Adverbs). In other words, we can create new words in the four open classes of words. We use nouns to *identify objects*; we use adjectives to *describe objects*; and we use adverbs to *describe actions*. Sometimes, we use word building merely to change a root word from one open class to another.

Nominalisation

We call the process of turning a verb into a noun *nominalisation*. We turn verbs into nouns through the technique of word building (see also Word Building above). We use verbs to identify *actions* and so nominalisation is the process of turning an *action* into a *concept*. We have seen nominalisation already when we looked at gerunds (see also Nouns).

Shortcut grammar tips for verbs

We can test a word to see if the word is a verb by putting the preposition *to* in front of the word. In other words, we can turn a verb into the verb's *infinitive* form. We can write *to walk* and *to type* but not *to car* or *to cat*.

We have a number of suffixes which we use to turn verbs into nouns. A suffix is a particle or part of a word which we add to the *end* of a word to change the word's meaning. I have listed these suffixes below.

Verb	Suffix	Noun
to condemn	-tion	condemna**tion**
to measure	-ment	measure**ment**
to ally	-ance	alli**ance**
to suspend	-ence/-ense	susp**ense**
to expose	-ure	expos**ure**
to wreck	-age	wreck**age**

Writing tips for verbs

Avoid splitting the infinitive verb with an adverb in formal business writing such as *to quickly write*. Instead, put the adverb *before* or *after* the infinitive verb such as *quickly to write* or *to write quickly*. However, remember also that currently grammarians consider the split infinitive to be a mark of poor style rather than a mark of poor grammar.

Put an adverb *before* or *after* the compound verb such as *desperately has been trying* or *has been trying desperately* to create a more formal tone in your writing. Putting an adverb inside a compound verb such as *has desperately been trying* or *has been trying desperately* will create a conversational tone in your writing. However, we always form negative compound verbs by putting the negative word *not* inside the compound verb. We *write has **not** been trying*.

Avoid misplacing the adverb of a sentence by attaching the adverb to the wrong verb (see also Adverbs). *John **only** cares for numbers* means that John does nothing else with numbers except care for them. *John cares for numbers **only*** means that John cares for nothing else except numbers.

Avoid contracting the verb to the subject of a sentence in formal business writing such as *I'll* and *you're*. However, contractions can be useful for informal business writing because contractions create a conversational tone.

Verb exercises

Essential exercise   Circle the verbs below. Remember to use the preposition *to* if you want to test whether the word is a verb. The word is a verb if we can *perform* the word as an action.

them	coach	blue	here	shall
chair	fold	her	fast	small
black	day	hope	green	will
you	up	your	fax	our
fear	mine	post	its	be
file	tall	any	week	buy
lunch	get	sit	long	he
click	door	clip	glass	need

Bridging exercise   Circle the verbs below. Remember to use the preposition *to* if you want to test whether the word is a verb. The word is a verb if we can *perform* the word as an action.

audit	lawyer	copy	notebook	yourselves
file away	advise	look after	minor	boycott
despatch	himself	commence	advice	frustrate
costings	smiling	anxious	quickly	present
fearful	exchange	index	perceive	internal
despair	mostly	delay	hostile	politely
program	larger	flawless	sliding	reactive
sanctions	receive	anxiety	sharpener	expect

Applied exercise   Circle the verbs below. Remember to use the preposition *to* if you want to test whether the word is a verb. The word is a verb if we can *perform* the word as an action.

barrister	personal	speedily	administrate	consequently
stock market	American	envelope	authorise	necessity
hopefully	unavoidable	frequently	correctly	subsequently
send away for	administrator	pigeon hole	mistaken	incompetent
Falkland Islands	pathetically	objectify	appraisal	inadvertent
delegate	attractive	pathetic	get-together	South Africa
chairperson	United States	aggravate	telephone	minimal
accountant	disinterested	emergency	programme	fatality

(For answers see pages 177–178)

1.8 **Adverbs**

The function of adverbs

We use adverbs to *describe verbs* so adverbs give us more information about *actions*. Adverbs are an open class of word which means that we can add infinitely to the number of adverbs.

We can remember the function of adverbs easily because the word *adverb* contains the word *verb*. Adverbs are always single words. We call adverbs which are phrases *adverbials*. A phrase is a group of words. I will explain more about adverbials below (see also Phrases and Clauses).

The types of adverbs

We have three main types of adverbs in English. We have *adverbs of time*, *adverbs of place*, and *adverbs of manner*. We also have three other types of adverbs in English. We have *adverbs of frequency*, *adverbs of direction*, and *adverbs of degree*.

Adverbs of frequency

We use adverbs of frequency to write about how often someone performs an action. Adverbs of frequency include *never*, *hardly ever*, *seldom*, *occasionally*, *frequently*, *often*, *usually*, and *always*.
*The proposal **never** applied.*

Adverbs of time

We use adverbs of time to write about *when* someone performs an action.
*She bought the company **yesterday**.*

Adverbs of place

We use adverbs of place to write about *where* someone performs an action.
*He put the package **there**.*

Adverbs of manner

We use adverbs of manner to write about *how* someone performs an action. Adverbs of manner usually end in the suffix *-ly* so adverbs of manner are easy to recognise. Suffixes are particles or parts of words which we put at the *end* of a root word to change the root word's meaning (see also Word Building on page 39). Adverbs of manner are the most common type of adverb in English.
*They decided **quickly**.*

Adverbs of direction We use adverbs of direction to write about the direction in which someone performs an action. We form adverbs of direction with the suffixes *–ward(s)* and *-wise*. Suffixes are particles or parts of words which we put at the *end* of a root word to change the root word's meaning (see also Word Building). The Americans tend to write *toward* while the British tend to write *towards*.
*Go **towards** the left and then turn right.*
*Turn the lever **clockwise**.*

Adverbs of degree We use adverbs of degree to write about the degree of intensity to which someone performs an action. We form adverbs of degree by using intensifiers such as *very* or *extremely*. Consequently, adverbs of degree usually consist of an intensifier and an adverb.
*We worked **very quickly**.*
*They did **extremely well** in the competition.*

Adverbs in compound adjectives We can use adverbs to form compound adjectives. We use adjectives to *describe* objects (see also Adjectives). A compound adjective is an adjective made of more than one word. We always hyphenate compound adjectives (see also Punctuation).
*A **highly**-skilled worker.*
*A **well**-considered proposal.*

Comparative adverbs We can use adverbs as comparisons. We use comparative adjectives to compare the qualities of one *object* to the qualities of another *object* (see also Adjectives). Consequently, we use comparative adverbs to compare the nature of one *action* to the nature of another *action*.

We can form comparative adverbs using the structure *as (adverb) as*. Furthermore, we can form comparative adverbs using the structure *(adverb) –er than* for adverbs made of one or two syllables. We also use the structure *more (adverb) than* for adverbs made of two or more syllables.
*Kim works **as competently** (adverb) **as** Francesca.*
*Thomas thinks **faster** (adverb) **than** Rupert.*
*Pierre designs **more beautifully** (adverb) **than** Craig.*

Superlative adverbs We can use adverbs as superlatives. We use superlative adjectives to compare the qualities of one *object* to the qualities of two or more other *objects* (see also Adjectives). Consequently, we use superlative adverbs to compare the nature of one *action* to the nature of two or more other *actions*.

We use the structure *the (adverb) -est* to compare adverbs made of one or two syllables. We also use the structure *the most (adverb)* to compare adverbs made of two or more syllables.
*Samantha thinks **the fastest** (adverb) out of the team. Vernon works **the most competently** (adverb) of the group.*

The position of adverbs

We can put adverbs at the *beginning*, *middle*, or *end* of a sentence.
***Yesterday**, Richard called and asked for a catalogue.*
*Richard called **yesterday** and asked for a catalogue.*
*Richard called and asked for a catalogue **yesterday**.*

Misplaced adverbs

We can change the meaning of a sentence if we *misplace* the adverb. We should keep our adverbs near to the verb whose action the adverb is describing.
*The group **quickly** decided to change their approach.*
*The group decided to change **quickly** their approach.*
*The group decided to change their approach **quickly**.*

The split infinitive

We say that we have *split the infinitive* when we put an adverb between the verb and the preposition *to* in an infinitive verb. An infinitive verb is a verb without a tense such as *to write* or *to speak* (see also Verbs). In other words, we do not know *when* an infinitive verb happens.

We should put the adverb either *before* or *after* the infinitive verb. However, splitting the infinitive is a mark of poor style rather than poor grammar.
*Write to **quickly** type as to type **quickly** or **quickly** to type.*

Compound verbs and adverbs

We should avoid putting an adverb in the middle of a compound verb. A compound verb is a verb made of more than one word (see also Verbs and Tense).
*Write has been **desperately** trying as has been trying **desperately** or **desperately** has been trying.*

Adverbials

We sometimes use phrases as adverbs. When a phrase describe *when*, *where*, or *how* we perform an action, then the phrase is an adverb.

Short cut grammar tips for adverbs

We can test a word to see if the word is an adverb by asking whether the word tells us *when*, *where*, or *how* we perform an action.

Adverbs of manner indicate how we perform actions and usually end in the suffix *–ly*.
Slowly, quickly, and courageously.

We call phrases which we use as adverbs *adverbials* (see also Phrases and Clauses).

Fayed met the client **in the afternoon** (adverbial of time).

Franco put the file **in the cabinet** (adverbial of place).

Soo Lin compiled the report **in a hurry** (adverbial of manner).

Word building   We use word building to create new words in English. We build new words by adding prefixes and suffixes to root words. We add prefixes to the *beginning* of root words and we add suffixes to the *end* of root words.

Un- (prefix) *plus* **comfort** (root word) *plus* **-able** (suffix) *equals* **uncomfortable**.

We can create new nouns, verbs, adjectives, and adverbs with word building (see also Nouns, Verbs, and Adjectives). In other words, we can create new words in the four open classes of words. We use nouns to *identify objects*; we use verbs to *identify actions*; and we use adjectives to *describe objects*. Sometimes we use word building merely to change a root word from one open class to another.

We always use certain suffixes to form root words into adverbs. I have listed below the suffixes which we use to form root words into adverbs.

Writing tips for adverbs   Avoid splitting the infinitive verb with an adverb in formal business writing such as *to quickly write*. Instead, put the adverb *before* or *after* the infinitive verb such as *quickly to write* or *to write quickly*. However, remember also that currently grammarians consider the split infinitive to be a mark of poor style rather than a mark of poor grammar.

Put an adverb *before* or *after* the compound verb such as **desperately** *has been trying* or *has been trying* **desperately** to create a more formal tone in your writing. Putting an adverb inside a compound verb such as *has* **desperately** *been trying* or *has been trying* **desperately** will create a more conversational tone in your writing. However, we always form negative compound verbs by putting the negative word *not* inside the compound verb. We *write has* **not** *been trying*.

Avoid misplacing the adverb of a sentence by attaching the adverb to the wrong verb (see also Adverbs). *John* **only** *cares for numbers* means that John does nothing else with numbers except care for them. *John cares for numbers* **only** means that John cares for nothing else except numbers.

Good is an adjective but not an adverb. However, *well* is an adverb and also an adjective. Finally, *deadly* is an adjective and *fatally* is an adverb.

Root word	Suffix	Adverb
slow	-ly	slowly
to	-ward(s)	toward(s)
clock	-wise	clockwise
fast	-er *plus* than	faster than
quick	the *plus* -est	the quickest

Adverb exercises

Essential exercise Circle the adverbs below. Remember that adverbs usually end in the suffix *-ly* but some adverbs are exceptions. Test the word by relating the word to a verb. An adverb will indicate *when*, *where*, or *how* we perform an action.

my	desk	keep	now	weekly
here	theirs	then	hers	we
yearly	him	team	daily	ever
fax	quickly	today	dine	may
big	book	cope	call	monthly
loosely	you	its	they	won't
white	well	good	shortly	there
stamp	ring	am	bind	was

Bridging exercise   Circle the adverbs below. Remember that adverbs usually end in the suffix *-ly* but some adverbs are exceptions. Test the word by relating the word to a verb. An adverb will indicate *when*, *where*, or *how* we perform an action.

ourselves	often	yourself	falling	before
lately	concede	perfectly	decide	Hong Kong
purchase	keyboard	afraid	only	caringly
purple	mostly	section	decade	customer
send out	call up	deeply	bigger	externally
happily	season	proof-read	paper	holdings
enjoy	quicker	touchy	out-tray	extension
represent	confident	willingly	photograph	slightly

Applied exercise   Circle the adverbs below. Remember that adverbs usually end in the suffix *-ly* but some adverbs are exceptions. Test the word by relating the word to a verb. An adverb will indicate *when*, *where*, or *how* we perform an action.

communication	abundantly	journalese	usually	courier
America	prejudice	annual	directorship	exceptionally
tomorrow	please	fearfully	stationery	competent
employee	Zimbabwe	relocation	counterfeit	distantly
perceptively	decidedly	naturally	administration	the largest
specialist	take-over	write away for	every	effectively
decisively	filing cabinet	authoritatively	English	India
Dow Jones Index	redistribution	melancholy	operationally	rationalise

(For answers see pages 178–179)

1.9 **Numerals**

The function and types of numbers

We use numerals to write about *numbers*. We have *three* types of numerals. We have *cardinal numbers*, *ordinal numbers*, and *fractional numbers*.

Cardinal numbers

We use cardinal numbers to write about *quantity*. Cardinal numbers are all numbers above, below, and including zero. Consequently, cardinal numbers are *infinite*. We use cardinal numbers to write about countable nouns which are nouns which we can form into plurals (see also Nouns).
*Four sections or **eight** team members.*

Ordinal numbers

We use ordinal numbers to write about *order* or *position in a sequence*.
First, second, third, fourth, fifth, sixth, seventh, eighth, ninth, and tenth.

Fractional numbers

We use fractional numbers or fractions to write about *quantities less than one and bigger than zero*. We *hyphenate* fractions when we use fractions to form *compound numbers*.
*A **half**, a **third**, a **quarter**, a **fifth**, a **sixth**, a **seventh**, an **eighth**, a **ninth**, and a **tenth**.*
Three-tenths, one-fifth, or six-ninths.

We can combine fractions with cardinal numbers. We hyphenate these numerals because they form *compound numbers*.
One-and-a-quarter or two-and-a-third.

Writing numbers as words and figures

We usually write cardinal numbers from *zero* to *ten* usually as words.
*We have bought **six** new chairs for the office.*

We usually write all cardinal numbers from *11* upwards usually as figures. However, we should avoid starting sentences with a figure. Consequently, we write all numbers as words when we start a sentence with a number.
*You will need about **15** minutes to complete the questionnaire.*
Nineteen people will attend the briefing next week.

Writing about time and dates

We can write about time in three ways.
Four o' clock.
4.00pm.
1600.

O' clock means *of the clock*. We use an apostrophe to show that we have contracted the words together (see also Punctuation).

We can write dates without any abbreviations.
6 July 2002.

We only need to use abbreviations if we have not referred to a month directly. We use abbreviations in this case to show that the numbers about which we are writing are dates and not quantities.
*We can have the meeting on the **22nd**, **23rd**, or **24th**.*

Writing tips for numerals

Write cardinal numbers *between zero and ten* as words.

Write cardinal numbers *from 11 onwards* as figures.

Always write a number as a word if the number *starts* a sentence.

Always *hyphenate* compound numerals or numbers made of *more than one* numeral.

Use no abbreviations for dates which *include* the month.

Use abbreviations for dates which *do not include* the month to indicate to your user that the figure is a date and not a quantity.

1.10 Conjunctions

The function of conjunctions

We use conjunctions to join sentences. Every sentence must have two components to be complete. A sentence must have a subject and a main verb. A subject is a noun which *performs* action of the main verb. A main or finite verb is a verb which has a tense or which tells us *when* an action happened (see also Sentences). We can have two subjects and two main verbs when we join two sentences. The subjects of the two sentences may or may not be the same.

The types of conjunctions

We have three ways of joining sentences in English. We can use conjunctions; conjunctive adverbs; or conjunctive phrases.

We can join sentences also with adverbs of time such as *before* or *after* (see also Adverbs).
Martin (subject) *finished* (main verb) *the presentation* (object) *months* **before** (adverb of time) *the conference* (subject) *took place* (main verb).

Conjunctions

We call conjunctions a closed class of word because we cannot create new words in this group. Below is a list of conjunctions and how these conjunctions function.

And	*Links* sentences and ideas. Shows a *causal* connection. In other words, one thing makes another thing happen.
But	Shows *contrast*.
Because	Gives a *reason*.
Or	Provides an *alternative*.
So	Gives a *reason*. Shows a *causal* connection. In other words, one thing makes another thing happen.
If	Suggests a conditional situation which can be *real* or *unreal*.

Writing tips for conjunctions	Some people think that we should not use a conjunction to start a sentence. However, we should consider starting a sentence with a conjunction as an issue of *style* rather than of *grammar*.

Consider the *effect* which starting a sentence with a conjunction will have on the tone of a piece of writing. Sentences which start with conjunctions seem more conversational. These sentences imitate spoken English and so are more informal.

Avoid starting a sentence with a conjunction in *formal* business writing, since the function of a conjunction is to join. Consider using a conjunctive adverb instead.
But (conjunction) *we should consider still the impact of the decision.*
However (conjunctive adverb), *we should consider still the impact of the decision.*

The exception to the guideline of not starting a sentence with a conjunction is the conjunction *if.* We use the conjunction *if* to join the conditional clause of a conditional sentence to the action clause (see also Modals and Conditionals).
If you have any questions (conditional clause), *please contact me on 0171 444 5555* (action clause).

Consequently, we can start a sentence acceptably with the conjunction *if* when the sentence is conditional. However, the sentence will be more direct if we put the action clause first and then the conditional clause. We can avoid starting a sentence with a conjunction also in this form.
Please contact me on 0171 444 5555 (action clause) *if you have any questions* (conditional clause).

Conjunctive adverbs	We also use conjunctive adverbs to join sentences. More importantly, conjunctive adverbs show how we fit *ideas* into a text. Consequently, we often call conjunctive adverbs *linking words*.

Conjunctive adverbs link ideas both between sentences and between paragraphs. Conjunctive adverbs can tell us about *time, place* or *manner* since conjunctive adverbs are adverbs which join sentences (see also Adverbs).

Furthermore, conjunctive adverbs often end in the suffix *–ly* since conjunctive adverbs are adverbs. Consequently, we can recognise some conjunctive adverbs easily. However, we have some exceptions to this rule such as *however* and *also*.

Conjunctive adverbs are different from conjunctions in two ways. Firstly, conjunctive adverbs are more formal. Secondly, conjunctive adverbs have a wider or more subtle range of meaning.

Below is a list of conjunctive adverbs. I have arranged the list according to how we use these adverbs.

Starting information in a list

firstly	mainly	principally

Adding information to a list or in general

secondly, etc	moreover	additionally
furthermore	also	equally

Finishing information in a list or in general

finally	lastly	eventually

Providing a concession to an idea

nevertheless	still	yet	however

Providing a result to an idea

consequently	so	therefore
then	since	otherwise

Providing an alternative to an idea

alternatively	conversely	instead

Other conjunctive adverbs

Conjunctive adverb	Meaning
namely	provides an example
rather	reformulates an idea
incidentally	provides an aside

Punctuation with conjunctive adverbs

We begin conjunctive adverbs with a capital letter and we follow the conjunctive adverbs with a comma when we start a sentence with a conjunctive adverb (see also Punctuation).

*We need the stock immediately. **However,** we only have storage space for half of the stock which we need.*

We end the first sentence with semi-colon; we start the conjunctive adverb with a small letter; and we follow the conjunctive adverb with a comma when we join two sentences with a conjunctive adverb (see also Punctuation).

*We need the stock immediately; **however,** we only have storage space for half of the stock which we need.*

Writing tips for conjunctive adverbs	We begin the conjunctive adverb with a capital letter and we follow the conjunctive adverb with a comma when we start a sentence with a conjunctive adverb. *We need the stock immediately. **However,** we only have storage space for half of the stock which we need.* We end the first sentence with semi-colon; we start the conjunctive adverb with a small letter; and we follow the conjunctive adverb with a comma when we join two sentences with a conjunctive adverb. *We need the stock immediately; **however,** we only have storage space for half of the stock which we need.* We use conjunctive adverbs to *start* sentences and to *join* sentences. However, we should try to avoid using conjunctive adverbs in the *middle* of sentences in formal business writing. Nevertheless, the position of a conjunctive adverb is an issue of *style* rather than of *grammar*. Putting a conjunctive adverb in the *middle* of a sentence is typical of spoken English. We can consider a conversational style as *inappropriate* to formal business writing (see also Style and Tone). We can argue that we should avoid putting a conjunctive adverb in the *middle* of a sentence since we would never put a conjunction in a similar position. *We need the stock immediately. We only have storage space, **however** (conjunctive adverb), for half of the stock which we need.* *We need the stock immediately. We only have storage space **but** (conjunction) for half of the stock which we need.*

Conjunctive phrases

Sometimes we join sentences and paragraphs with phrases rather than words. These phrases also show the *relationship* between ideas. Conjunctive phrases are useful also for signposting the user so that the user knows where he or she is in relation to the material. Conjunctive phrases also create *flow* within a text (see also Style and Tone).

Below is a list of conjunctive phrases. I have arranged the list according to how we use these phrases.

Starting information in a list

first of all	for one thing	in the first place

Adding information to a list or in general

in addition	what is more	above all

Finishing information in a list or in general

in conclusion	to conclude	to sum up

Developing ideas

for example	for instance	that is to say

Providing a concession to an idea

in any case	all the same
in spite of that	at any rate

Providing a contrast to an idea

on the contrary	on the other hand

Reformulating an idea

put differently	in that case	in other words

Providing a result to an idea

as a result	in that case

Writing tips for conjunctive phrases

Use conjunctive phrases to start sentences and always end a conjunctive phrase with a comma (see also Phrases and Clauses and Punctuation).
On the other hand, we should consider carefully how our competitors will respond.

Avoid separating subjects and main verbs with a conjunctive phrase (see also Nouns and Verbs and Sentences). Instead, put the conjunctive phrase in the *first* position of the sentence and keep the subject and main verb together.
The team (subject), **as a result**, *needs* (main verb) *to work harder.*
As a result, *the team* (subject) *needs* (main verb) *to work harder.*

Avoid separating compound verbs with a conjunctive phrase (see also Verbs). Instead, put the conjunctive phrase in the *first* position of the sentence and keep the compound verb together.
The department **has**, *in other words,* **been developing** (compound verb) *a new system.*
In other words, the department **has been developing** (compound verb) *a new system.*

1.11 **Review**

The types of words

So far we have looked at the words which we use to create language. Initially, we established that we have open classes of words and closed classes of words. We can create new words in the open classes but the closed classes are fixed. The open classes include nouns, verbs, adjectives, and adverbs. The closed classes include pronouns; prepositions; articles and determiners; and conjunctions.

The two main word groups

We looked then at words in the form of the two main groups. We established that we use the noun group of words to write about *objects*. Furthermore, we use the verb group of words to write about *actions*. We saw also that each of the main groups of words has a number of related words.

The noun and the verb groups

Under the noun group of words, we looked at the types of nouns; the types of pronouns; the types of adjectives; prepositions; and articles and determiners. Under the verb group of words, we looked only at the types of verbs and the types of adverbs. We will look at verb conjugation and tense after we have looked at sentences in Section Two.

Same words with different functions

We also saw how we can use the same word as either a noun or as a verb. We established that we can analyse sentences more effectively if we think about how words *function* in sentences rather than about what words *mean*. Grammar and meaning are two separate issues in language. We call the study of meaning *semantics*. We will explore the differences between grammar and meaning further when we look at sentences.

Word building

We looked at word building to explore how we can change the *meaning* of words by creating new words. We saw that we build new words by adding particles or parts of words to root words. We add prefixes to the *front* of a root word and we add suffixes to the *end* of a root word. We identified *nominalisation* as the process of building a verb into a noun. We established that nominalisation is particularly relevant to style and tone in business writing.

Putting words into groups

Finally, we looked at conjunctions which provide us with an appropriate lead into the next section of The Workbook. In Section Two, we will look at how we put words into groups such as phrases, clauses, and sentences. More importantly, we will look at the types of *meaning* which we can create with these groups of words.

PART TWO

Groups of words

2.1 **Preview**

The two primary functions of words

We looked in Part One at words which are some of the smallest components of language. We looked at how we use words to define the world around us. We established that the most important information which we communicate to other people is about *objects* and *actions*. Now we are going to look at how we group words to provide more detailed information for other people. Significantly, we will start focusing more on meaning now.

The function of phrases and clauses

We will start by looking at phrases and clauses. We have encountered phrases already when we looked at the open classes of words. In *the parts of speech* we explored noun phrases; predicative adjectives; verb phrases; and adverbials. We examined also prepositional phrases and conjunctive phrases. Now we will distinguish phrases from clauses and we will look also at the role of clauses in constructing some forms of sentences.

The types and functions of sentences

Then we will establish what makes a sentence different from a phrase or a clause. We will focus on the three main types of sentences as well as which types are most appropriate for business writing. Nevertheless, we will look primarily at what a sentence needs to be complete. We touched on main verbs and on subject and object nouns when we looked at the open classes of words. Now we will look in more detail at how subjects, main verbs, and objects *function* in sentences. More importantly, we will look at how the function of subjects, main verbs, and objects affects us as business writers.

The function of verb conjugation and tense

At that point, we will look at verb conjugation and tense although strictly these two aspects of grammar belong to *the parts of speech*. However, I have chosen to discuss verb conjugation and tense in *groups of words* since conjugation and tense are relevant to constructing complete sentences. Consequently, we will establish clearly the guidelines for using the simple, continuous, and perfect tenses.

Subject and verb agreement

Then we will spend some time looking at a rule of grammar called subject and verb agreement. We will identify the mistakes which we are likely to make with agreement in business writing and also at why we are likely to make these agreement mistakes.

Active and passive voice

Moreover, we will look at active and passive voice while we are looking at subjects and verbs. We will establish why voice is a feature of style and how voice affects the tone of our business writing. We will identify also the situations where the active and the passive voice are most appropriate.

Modal verbs and conditional sentences

The last aspects of sentences at which we will look will be modal verbs and conditional sentences. Modal verbs also strictly belong to *the parts of speech*. However, I have chosen to discuss modals in *groups of words* because modals are relevant to conditional sentences. We have looked already at modals briefly under Verbs in *the parts of speech*. However, we will identify how we use modal verbs to create different meanings in different sentences in *groups of words*. We will identify also some of the types of conditional sentences and the situations in which we are likely to use conditionals.

Direct and indirect speech

Finally, we will look at direct and indirect speech. We could see writing about what other people have said as an aspect of punctuation. However, I have chosen to include direct and indirect speech under *groups of words* because using the speech of others is another way in which we can create sentences. Indirect speech is particularly relevant to people who take and write minutes and to people who create press releases. From speech, we will be ready to start looking at how we put sentences into paragraphs. However, we will look at paragraphs in detail in Part Three only.

2.2 **Phrases and clauses**

The function of phrases

We can define a phrase as a group of words which makes sense but which has no main verb. A verb is a word which identifies an *action* (see also Verbs). A main verb is a verb which identifies an action and a tense or *when* an action happened. Consequently, a phrase is a group of words which provides information but which is not a sentence.

*A group **of experienced consultants** (phrase) compiled the proposal.*

The types of phrases

We have encountered several phrase types in Part One. We have explored noun phrases; adjectival phrases or predicative adjectives; prepositional phrases; verb phrases; adverbials; and conjunctive phrases.

Noun phrases

We call a group of words which tells us more information about a noun *a noun phrase*. A noun is a word which identifies an *object* (see also Nouns). Noun phrases often contain articles, adjectives, and prepositions. Consequently, we can classify noun phrases also as prepositional phrases or adjectival phrases.

The narrow, wooden table (noun phrase) *is on sale.*
The goals of the team (noun phrase) *are stretching.*

We make subject and verb agreement errors often when we write complex noun phrases. The rule of subject and verb agreement says that the subject and the main verb of a sentence *must agree with each other in **number*** (see also Subject and Verb Agreement). Sometimes we agree the main verb with the *wrong* noun in the noun phrase.

The goal (subject) *of the teams* (prepositional or adjectival phrase) ***is*** (main verb) *stretching.*

Adjectival phrases

We call a group of words which *describes* an object *an adjectival phrase*. Adjectives are words which we use to *describe* objects (see also Adjectives). An adjectival phrase often follows an intransitive verb. An intransitive verb is a verb which describes an action which we *cannot transfer* to another object. Consequently, intransitive verbs usually describe *states of being*. Examples of intransitive verbs include the verbs *to be, to seem*, and *to appear* (see also Verbs).

*The committee is **evenly-divided*** (adjectival phrase).
The evenly-divided committee (noun phrase) *met yesterday*.

Prepositional phrases

We call a group of words which follows a preposition *a prepositional phrase*. Prepositions are words which tell us about the *position* or *movement* of objects.
*The company is moving **to the city*** (prepositional phrase).
*We put the information **through the system*** (prepositional phrase).

Verb phrases

We call a group of words which tells us more information about a verb *a verb phrase*. Consequently, verb phrases often contain adverbs. Verbs are words which we use to identify *actions* (see also Verbs). Adverbs are words which we use to describe *when*, *where*, or *how* we perform actions (see also Adverbs).

Verb phrases can include also phrasal verbs and compound verbs. Phrasal verbs are verbs which we create with a verb and one or more prepositions. Prepositions are words which we use to indicate the *position* or *movement* of objects (see also Prepositions). Compound verbs are verbs which are made of a verb and one or more auxiliary verbs. Auxiliary verbs are verbs which help main verbs. The three auxiliary verbs are *to be*, *to do*, and *to have* (see also Verbs).
*The engineer **surveyed the property thoroughly over a six-week period*** (verb phrase).
*The team **is breaking up*** (phrasal verb).
*We **have been monitoring** the signal system for four months* (compound verb).

Adverbials

We call a group of words which describes a verb *an adverbial*. A verb is a word which we use to *identify* an action (see also Verbs). An adverb is a word which we use to *describe* actions (see also Adverbs). Adverbs tell us *when*, *where*, or *how* we perform an action. Adverbial phrases of place often begin with a preposition. A preposition is a word which we use to indicate the *position* or *movement* of an object (see also Prepositions).
*We moved the equipment **yesterday before lunch*** (adverbial of time).
*We moved the equipment **to the corner of the warehouse*** (adverbial of place).
*We moved the equipment **slowly and carefully*** (adverbial of manner).

Conjunctive phrases

We call a group of words which we use to join sentences *a conjunctive phrase* (see also Conjunctions). We use conjunctive phrases to *signpost* our user. In other words, we use conjunctive phrases to show our user how the ideas in our text fit together.

On the other hand (conjunctive phrase), *we could re-evaluate the system.*

The function of clauses

We use clauses to form complex sentences (see also Sentences). We use complex sentences to write about ideas which we have *integrated* into each other and not merely *joined* with a conjunction such as *and* (see also Conjunctions).

A clause is a group of words with a main verb. A main verb is a verb which identifies both an *action* and a *tense* (see also Verbs). However, a clause typically has no subject unlike a sentence. A subject is a noun which *performs* the action of the main verb (see also Nouns and Sentences). Consequently, we can describe a clause as a *partial* sentence which cannot stand alone. In other words, a clause relies on the subject of the sentence in which the clause is integrated to make sense.

The types of clauses

We have explored a number of clause types in The Workbook. We have examined defining relative clauses; non-defining relative clauses (see also Relative Pronouns); main clauses; subordinate clauses (see also Sentences); action clauses; and condition clauses (see also Modals and Conditionals).

Defining relative clauses

We call a clause which provides extra information and which defines the subject of a sentence a *defining relative clause*. Consequently, we also call defining relative clauses *identifying relative clauses*. Defining relative clauses begin with a relative pronoun such as *who*, *which*, or *that* (see also Relative Pronouns). We never use commas to insert a defining relative clause into a sentence (see also Punctuation).
*The man **who sold the equipment to us*** (defining relative clause) *was unavailable.*

Non-defining relative clauses

We call a clause which provides extra information but which does not define the subject of a sentence a *non-defining relative clause*. Consequently, we also call non-defining relative clauses *non-identifying relative clauses*. Non-defining relative clauses also begin with a relative pronoun such as *who*, *which*, or *that* (see also Relative Pronouns). We always use commas to insert a non-defining relative clause into a sentence (see also Punctuation).
*Khimji, **who originated the idea for the project**, left the team half-way through the design stage.*

Main clauses

We call the *most important idea* in a complex sentence *the main clause* of the sentence. A complex sentence is a simple sentence with at least one other clause (see also Sentences).

The team project manager agreed the team members (main clause)
before we compiled the data (subordinate clause).

Subordinate clauses

We call the *least important idea* in a complex sentence *the subordinate clause* of the sentence. A complex sentence is a simple sentence with at least one other clause (see also Sentences).
The team project manager agreed the team members (main clause) **before we compiled the data** (subordinate clause).

Action clauses

We call a clause which identifies the action in a conditional sentence *the action clause*. The action clause tells us which action the subject should perform if the conditions are right. We often write the action clause in the imperative mood (see also Sentences). We use the imperative mood to give *commands* or *instructions*.
Put the equipment on the table (action clause in the imperative mood) *if you have no space on the floor* (condition clause).

We use conditional sentences to write about both *real* and *unreal or hypothetical* situations. We have four types of conditional sentences although some grammarians identify other types. The four types are *zero, first, second,* and *third conditional* (see also Modals and Conditionals).

Condition clauses

We call the clause which identifies the *necessary condition* in a conditional sentence *a condition clause*. The condition clause tells us which condition needs to exist in order for the subject to perform a particular action. Consequently, the condition clause begins with the conjunction *if*. We use conjunctions to join sentences (see also Conjunctions).
Put the equipment on the table (action clause) **if you have no space on the floor** (condition clause).

We use conditional sentences to write about both *real* and *unreal or hypothetical* situations. We have four types of conditional sentences although some grammarians identify other types. The four types are *zero, first, second,* and *third conditional* (see also Modals and Conditionals).

Writing tips for phrases and clauses

Be aware of creating complex subjects when you use phrases to provide extra information about the subject of a sentence. A complex subject is a subject made of a phrase or a clause rather than a word. Using complex subjects can lead easily to mistakes with subject and verb agreement.

Always use a comma after a conjunctive phrase (see also Punctuation).

Avoid using non-defining relative clauses because these clauses separate the subject and the main verb of a sentence. Instead, use the non-defining relative clause as a separate sentence.

Put the main clause of a complex sentence first and then follow with the subordinate clause. The sentence will be more direct with the main clause in the first position.

Put the action clause before the condition clause in a conditional sentence. The sentence will be more direct with the action clause in the first position. Moreover, you also will avoid starting the sentence with the conjunction *if*.

2.3 **Sentences**

The function of sentences

A sentence is a unit of information which provides a *message*. The message of a sentence is that someone or something performs an action at a particular time. That person or thing may have performed that action on someone or something else but not necessarily. Consequently, a sentence must have at least two elements to be complete. A complete sentence must have a subject and a predicate.

The subject and predicate of a sentence

We can divide a sentence into the subject and the predicate. The subject *performs* the action of the sentence. The predicate is the rest of the sentence other than the subject. A predicate must have a main verb to be complete. A main verb tells us which action the subject performs and the tense of that action (see also Nouns and Verbs). The tense tells us *when* the subject performs the action.

A predicate can include also either a predicative adjective or an object. We follow an intransitive verb with a predicative adjective (see also Adjectives). An intransitive verb is a verb which cannot take an object such as the verb *to be*. We use intransitive verbs to indicate *states of being* (see also Verbs).

An object is a noun which *receives* the action of the main verb. We call a main verb which we can transfer to an object *a transitive verb*. Transitive verbs usually tell us about *actions*. However, not all verbs which describe actions are transitive verbs such as *to walk*.

We need only a subject and a main verb for a sentence to be complete. However, a sentence usually needs a predicate to communicate a *message* effectively.
The team (subject) *is motivated* (predicate).
The team (subject) *is* (intransitive main verb) *motivated* (predicative adjective).
The staff members (subject) *are eating their lunch* (predicate).
The staff members (subject) *are eating* (transitive main verb) *their lunch* (object).

The subject, main verb, and object of a sentence

The nouns and the verbs of a sentence have a relationship to each other. The main verb of a sentence is the verb which identifies *an action* and *a tense*. The tense identifies *when* something happened (see also Verbs and Tense).

Some nouns *perform* the action of the main verb. We call these nouns the subject of the sentence. Some nouns *receive* the action of the main verb. We call these nouns the object of the sentence. A noun is a word we use to identify things (see also Nouns).

Direct and indirect objects

The direct object of a sentence *directly receives* the action of the main verb. We follow a transitive main verb with an object. A transitive verb is a verb which can take an object (see also Verbs). *We* (subject) *invested* (transitive verb) *the surplus* (direct object).

The indirect object of a sentence *indirectly receives* the action of the main verb. In other words, the indirect object is the *second* recipient of the action of the main verb.
I (subject) *gave* (transitive main verb) *him* (indirect object) *the ultimatum* (direct object).

The types of sentences

We have three types of sentences in English. The three types are *simple*, *compound,* and *complex sentences*.

Simple sentences

Simple sentences have at least a subject and a main verb. The main verb can be either transitive or intransitive. A simple sentence can have also *two* other components. A simple sentence can have a direct object if the verb is transitive. Furthermore, a simple sentence can have a predicative adjective if the verb is intransitive (see also Nouns and Verbs and Adjectives).
We (subject) *held* (transitive main verb) *the meeting* (object) *on Thursday*.
Gwen (subject) *felt* (intransitive main verb) *confident about winning the contract* (predicative adjective).

Compound sentences

We create compound sentences by joining two or more simple sentences. A simple sentence has at least a subject and a main verb (see also Nouns and Verbs). We join compound sentences with a conjunction or a conjunctive adverb (see also Conjunctions). Consequently, compound sentences can have two or more subjects and

Short cut grammar tip for direct and indirect objects

Rewrite the sentence in the passive voice if you have difficulty in identifying the direct and indirect object of a sentence. The order of a passive sentence is object, main verb, and subject (see also Active and Passive Voice).

I (subject) *gave* (transitive main verb) *him* (indirect object) *the ultimatum* (direct object).
The ultimatum (direct object) *was given* (transitive passive main verb) *to him* (indirect object) *by me* (subject).

two or more main verbs. A compound sentence can have also two or more objects if the main verbs are transitive (see also Nouns and Verbs). Conjunctions include *and, but, because, or, so,* and *if.* Conjunctive adverbs include *moreover, however, consequently,* and *alternatively. We* (subject) *held* (transitive main verb) *the meeting* (object) *on Thursday* **but** (conjunctive) *not everyone* (subject) *attended* (main verb). *Gwen* (subject) *felt* (intransitive main verb) *confident about winning the contract* (predicative adjective); **however** (conjunctive adverb), *the client* (subject) *never came back* (intransitive main verb) *to her as she had expected.*

We also can join sentences with an adverb of time such as *before* or *after* (see also Adverbs).
John called the engineer **after** *we had identified the problem.*

Complex sentences

We create complex sentences by putting two or more clauses into a simple or compound sentence. In other words, a complex sentence will have a main clause and one or more subordinate clauses (see also Phrases and Clauses). A main clause can be either a simple or a compound sentence. A simple sentence has at least a subject and a main verb (see also Nouns and Verbs). A compound subject is two or more simple sentences joined with a conjunction such as *and* (see also Conjunctions).

Subordinate clauses provide extra information about the main clause of a sentence. We often use relative pronouns to introduce subordinate clauses (see also Pronouns).
Bhavesh, who had thought of the original idea (non-identifying relative clause), *wanted to be responsible for the client but we decided instead to appoint a different account manager* (compound sentence).

Embedding

Embedding is a phrase, a clause, or even a sentence which *separates* the subject and the main verb of another sentence. Embedding makes the message of a sentence difficult to process since we cannot connect the subject and the main verb immediately.
Jasmine (subject), **without considering the consequences** (embedded phrase), *agreed* (main verb) *the schedule for the project.*

The imperative mood

We use the imperative mood to give *commands* or *instructions*. We call this type of sentence a *mood* because we create the tone of a command in a sentence by using a particular grammatical structure. The tone of a sentence is the *emotion* in the words (see also Style and Tone).

Limit your sentences to *one or two ideas* since long sentences are difficult to understand. In other words, write in simple and compound sentences. Another guideline would be to limit your sentences to *between twelve and eighteen words* since shorter sentences are easier to process.

Put the subject and verb in the *first position* in the sentence whenever possible. Keep the subject and the verb together and put extra information at the end of the sentence. In other words, avoid embedding extra information between the subject and the main verb. Put the *main idea* first as the main clause and then put the *supporting idea* in the second position as the subordinate clause (see also Phrases and Clauses).

Use the imperative mood for *instructions* and *procedures*. Use the word *please* to create a more personal tone if necessary (see also Style and Tone).

Imperative mood sentences are grammatically correct sentences even though these sentences have no clearly-visible subject. Instead, we *imply* the subject of the sentence since by definition someone or something must perform a main verb. The subject of an imperative mood sentence is always the second person. In other words, we imply always the subject pronoun *you* in an imperative mood sentence (see also Pronouns). We imply also the modal verb *must* since the sentence is a command or an instruction (see also Verbs).
Close (main verb) *the door and clear* (main verb) *the room* (imperative mood sentence).
You (subject) *must* (modal verb) *close* (main verb) *the door and clear* (main verb) *the room*.

General sentence exercise

Change the following groups of words into complete sentences if necessary.

1. Further to your letter of 8 January 2001.

---

2. Thank you for your prompt reply.

---

3. Stationery including paper, envelopes, and stamps.

---

4. Thanking you in advance.

5. Lift the cover and adjust the dial.

_____

6. No smoking please.

_____

7. Rising costs have forced the business to close.

_____

8. The team of specialists and support staff.

_____

9. Well-done, team.

_____

10. The end of year results showing a fall in profits with a full explanation below.

(For answers see page 180)

2.4 Tense

The function of tense   We use verbs to identify *actions* (see also Verbs). Furthermore, we use tense to identify *when* an action took place. In English, we encode the main verb of a sentence with the tense of the sentence. Not all languages use this system. The main verb of a sentence is the verb which identifies the action which the subject of the sentence *performs*. The subject of a sentence is the noun which identifies the person or thing who performs the action of the main verb (see also Nouns).

We have established that the main verb of a sentence identifies both an *action* and a *tense*. As a result, each sentence will have only one main verb. All subsequent verbs will identify actions only. Consequently, all subsequent verbs will be infinitive verbs (see also Verbs). An infinitive verb is a verb which identifies an *action* only and so has no tense. An example of an infinitive verb is the verb *to write*. We can have as many infinitive verbs as we need in a sentence to express our message.
The team (subject) **met** (main verb) **to create** (infinitive verb) *a plan of action* **to follow** (infinitive verb) *in the next quarter*.

The types of tenses   We have three main tenses in English. We have the *past*, the *present*, and the *future tenses*. Furthermore, we can divide each of these three main tenses into three other forms. The three other forms are the *simple*, the *continuous*, and the *perfect tenses*.

We form the tenses according to the *type* and the *number* of actions which take place. In other words, we use tense to communicate certain information to other people just as we use all aspects of grammar. Specifically, we use tense to communicate information about time and the number and order of actions which take place.

The infinitive verb   The infinitive verb is a verb without a tense. The infinitive is the *concept* of an action without a time (see also Verbs). The infinitive verb is preceded usually by the preposition *to* such as *to buy* or *to sell* (see also Prepositions). However, the infinitive verb has no preposition *to* after a modal verb such as *could be* or *might be* (see also Verbs). A modal verb is a verb which *modifies* or *changes* the action of the main verb. We use modals verbs to write about *possibility*, *certainty*, *intention*, and *permission* (see also Modals and Conditionals).

The simple tenses

Infinitive	Past	Present	Future
to go	he *went*	he *goes*	he *will go*

We use the simple tense to write about actions which *occur and finish* at a particular point in time. Consequently, we should use a *specific time reference* such as *yesterday* or *next week* when we use the simple tense. The time reference should be clear from the context of the writing if we use no specific time reference in our sentence.

The past simple tense

We use the past simple tense to write about an event which *occurred and finished* in the past. This event occurred and finished at a specific time. We always use a *specific time reference* when using the past simple tense. The time reference should be clear from the context of the writing if we use no specific time reference in our sentence.

We conjugate or form the past simple tense by putting the past participle on the *end* of the main verb of a sentence. The past participle is the suffix *–ed*. A suffix is a particle which we put on the *end* of a word (see also Word Building in Nouns and Verbs).
He **used** (main verb – past simple) *the profit to secure the loan.*

However, some verbs are *irregular* and so we change the verb's entire form to indicate the past simple tense.
We **bought** (main verb – irregular past simple) *the stock last month.*

The present simple tense

We use the present simple tense to write about an event which *occurs and finishes* in the present. We also use this tense to write about things which are *always true* or which *always should happen*. Consequently, we use the present simple tense for writing procedures.

The third person singular takes always the suffix *–s* in the present tense. A suffix is a particle which we put on the *end* of a word (see also Word Building in Nouns and Verbs). We can test this rule by writing: *he types* but *you type*; or *she runs* but *they run* (see also Verb Conjugation).
We **keep** (main verb – present simple tense) *the stationery on the third floor.*

We use also the present simple tense to write about *future* events. However, we can use also the future simple tense.

*The committee **meets** (main verb – present simple tense) in four months time.*

*The committee **will meet** (main verb – future simple tense) in four months time.*

The future simple tense
We use the future simple tense to write about an event which will *happen and finish* in the future. We always use the modal verb *will* to form the future tenses. We use also the modal verb *will* to indicate that we *intend* to do something if the conditions are right (see also Modals and Conditionals).

*The new head of department **will join** (main verb – future simple tense) us in May.*

We can use the present simple tense also to write about future events.

*The new head of department **joins** (main verb – present simple tense) us in May.*

The continuous tenses

Infinitive	Past	Present	Future
to think	she *was thinking*	she *is thinking*	she *will be thinking*

We use the continuous tense to write about actions which are *in progress* at a particular point in time. Consequently, we should use a *specific time reference* such as *yesterday* or *next week* when we use the continuous tense. The time reference should be clear from the context of our writing if we use no specific time reference in our sentence.

We conjugate or form the continuous tense with the auxiliary verb *to be*; an infinitive verb without the preposition *to*; and the present participle –*ing*.

To be *plus* **think** *plus* **-ing** *equals* **to be thinking**.

The auxiliary verb *to be* is first and carries the tense of the continuous verb. An auxiliary verb is a verb which helps the main verb of a sentence (see also Verbs). We have only *three* auxiliary verbs in English which are *to be*, *to do*, and *to have*. The auxiliary verb usually carries the tense of the main verb.

The present participle is the suffix –*ing*. A suffix is a particle which we put on the *end* of a root word (see also Word Building in Nouns and Verbs).

The auxiliary verb, the infinitive verb, and the present participle form a complete verb. We call verbs made of more than one word *compound verbs* (see also Verbs).

The perfect tenses We can use both the simple and the continuous tenses in the perfect tense. The perfect tenses are not more grammatically correct than the simple or continuous tenses. Instead, we use the perfect tenses to write about different forms of time. We use the present perfect tense to write about events which began in the past and are relevant to the present. We use the past and future perfect tenses to write about more than one event in either the past or the future.

The perfect simple tenses

Infinitive	Past	Present	Future
to go	he *had gone*	he *has gone*	he *will have gone*

We conjugate the perfect tense by using: the auxiliary verb *to have*; the infinitive verb without the preposition *to*; and the past participles -*en*, -*ne*, or -*ed*. The auxiliary verb *to have* carries the tense of the verb.
To have plus *to be* plus –*en* equals *to have been*.
To have plus *to go* plus –*ne* equals *to have gone*.
To have plus *to talk* plus –*ed* equals *to have talked*.
To have plus *to meet* equals *to have met* (irregular).

The present perfect tense We use the present perfect tense to write about events which *occurred in the past* but which are *relevant to the present*. However, these events have *no specific time reference* unlike the past simple tense. These events occur at an *unspecified point* in the past.
*I **went*** (main verb – past simple) *to Asia **last year*** (specific time reference).
*I **have been*** (main verb – present perfect) *to Asia **twice*** (unspecific time reference).

The past perfect tense We use the past perfect tense to write about *the past in the past*. Consequently, we use the past perfect tense together with the past simple tense. We use the past simple tense to write about a specific past event. Furthermore, we use the past perfect tense to write about an event which occurred before that past simple event. We *imply* the past simple event if we do not use the past simple tense in the sentence.

Unfortunately, we **had paid** (past perfect) *already for the stock when we* **found** (past simple) *a cheaper supplier.*

The future perfect tense

We use the future perfect tense to write about *the future in the future*. Consequently, we also use the future perfect tense together with another tense. However, in this case we can use the future perfect tense together with the present simple tense or the present perfect tense. The future perfect tense refers to an event which will have occurred before another future event.

We **will have finished** (future perfect tense) *the collection by the time that the season* **starts** (present simple) *next month.*

I **will have returned** (future perfect tense) *by the time that you* **have gone** (present perfect tense).

The perfect continuous tenses

Infinitive	Past	Present	Future
to think	she *had been thinking*	she *has been thinking*	she *will have been thinking*

We conjugate or form the perfect continuous tense by using: the auxiliary verb *to have*; the auxiliary verb *to be* and the past participle *-en* which form *been*; the infinitive verb without the preposition *to*; and the present participle *-ing*. The auxiliary verb *to have* carries the tense of the verb.

To have *plus* **to be** *plus* **–en** *plus* **work** *plus* **–ing** *equals* **to have been working**.

We use the perfect continuous tense in the same way in which we use the continuous tense and the perfect tense. We use the perfect continuous tense to refer to an event in the past or the future which is *in progress at a particular time* and which is interrupted by a second event.

She **had been working** (past perfect continuous) *on the contract when the client* **called** (past simple).

He **will have been working** (future perfect continuous tense) *on the project for three months by the time that we* **assemble** (present simple) *the team.*

We use the present perfect continuous tense like the present perfect tense. We use the present perfect continuous tense to write about

<table>
<tr><td>**Short cut grammar tip for tense**</td><td>Verbs which follow the third person singular pronouns *he/she/it* always end in the suffix –*s* in the present tense only.
He writes; she directs; and it cleans.</td></tr>
</table>

<table>
<tr><td>**Writing tips for tense**</td><td>Avoid separating compound verbs with adverbs in writing formal business.
*Catherine **has been** desperately **trying** to finish the project.*
*Catherine **has** desperately **been trying** to finish the project.*

Instead, put the adverb before or after the compound verb.
*Catherine **has been trying** desperately to finish the project.*
*Catherine **has been trying** to finish the project desperately.*
(See also Compound Verbs and Adverbs).</td></tr>
</table>

events in the past which have *no specific time reference*. We also use the present perfect continuous tense to write about an event which was *in progress* at that unspecified time.

*They **have been preparing** (present perfect continuous) the material for three days*.

Tense exercises

Initial tense exercises Conjugate the auxiliary verb *to be* in the simple tense.

Person	Past	Present	Future
I	*was*	*am*	*will be*
You			
He/she/it			
We			
You			
They			

Conjugate the auxiliary verb *to be* in the continuous tense.

Person	Past	Present	Future
I	*was being*	*am being*	*will be being*
You			
He/she/it			
We			
You			
They			

Conjugate the auxiliary verb *to do* in the simple tense.

Person	Past	Present	Future
I	*did*	*do*	*will do*
You			
He/she/it			
We			
You			
They			

Conjugate the auxiliary verb *to do* in the continuous tense.

Person	Past	Present	Future
I	*was doing*	*am doing*	*will be doing*
You			
He/she/it			
We			
You			
They			

Conjugate the auxiliary verb *to have* in the simple tense.

Person	Past	Present	Future
I	*had*	*have*	*will have*
You			
He/she/it			
We			
You			
They			

Conjugate the auxiliary verb *to have* in the continuous tense.

Person	Past	Present	Future
I	*was having*	*am having*	*will be having*
You			
He/she/it			
We			
You			
They			

Essential exercises

Rewrite the following sentences so that the verbs are in the correct tense. Remember that a sentence can contain more than one verb. However, one of those verbs must be a main verb. The main verb of a sentence tells us two things: *what* happened and *when* that action happened. In other words, a main verb must have a tense. All subsequent verbs will be in the infinitive tense.

1. Denise (to book) the tickets tomorrow.

   _____

2. The courier (to deliver) the package last week.

   _____

3. The supplier (to deliver) the groceries everyday at 10am.

   _____

4. I (to enclose) a brochure and an order form for you (to consider).

   _____

5. We (to send) the new package last week but nothing (to arrive) yet.

6. We (to send) the new package last week but nothing (to arrive) until yesterday.

_____

7. I (to fax) joining instructions last week for you (to look at) before you (to leave) next Tuesday.

_____

8. I (to think) about you when you (to call) yesterday because I (to not be able) (to find) your order form.

Bridging exercises Rewrite the following sentences so that the verbs are in the correct tense. Remember that a sentence can contain more than one verb. However, one of those verbs must be a main verb. The main verb of a sentence tells us two things: _what_ happened and _when_ that action happened. In other words, a main verb must have a tense. All subsequent verbs will be in the infinitive tense.

9. We (to visit) the clients twice but the clients (to not decide) yet whether (to use) our services.

_____

10. You (to must cancel) all tickets within at least fourteen working days from the date of issue if you (to want) a refund.

_____

11. The magazine (to print) the article a fortnight ago while he (to travel) abroad. Consequently, he (to not see) nor (to read) anything yet.

_____

12. You (to must save) the material while you (to work) still on the file. Otherwise, you (to lose) all the work you (to complete) if the power (to fail) unexpectedly.

_____

13. We (to must not underestimate) the difficulty of this situation. We (to can not assume) that our competitors (to not grasp) the opportunity if they (to come) (to hear) of anything.

14. We (to expect) the client (to call) yesterday. However, the client (to not call) and we (to not be able) (to reach) him since then. In the meantime, we (to continue) (to work) on the proposal.

15. We (to have) (to remove) the walls before we (to can begin) constructing the foundations. In fact, we (to lay) still the foundations and we (to not expect) (to finish) until next month.

16. The company (to consider) the option of recruiting new staff before the merger (to occur) last year. However, we now (to decide) instead (to decrease) our production for the time being as this tactic (to be) more cost effective.

Applied exercises Rewrite the following sentences so that the verbs are in the correct tense. Remember that a sentence can contain more than one verb. However, one of those verbs must be a main verb. The main verb of a sentence tells us two things: *what* happened and *when* that action happened. In other words, a main verb must have a tense. All subsequent verbs will be in the infinitive tense.

17. Abdul (to be) responsible for managing over twenty members of staff and (to create) a 20% increase in production while he (to work) for this section. We (to think) of promoting him again when he (to announce) his decision (to leave).

18. The department (to use) the current system for four years by the time that the new system (to come) into place next year. Unfortunately, we (to buy) the new system before we (to learn) that we (to move) to a larger location in the city next autumn.

19. We (to be) concerned over the last four months about your attendance at work. We (to would like) (to speak) to you about this situation before the end of the month. I (to need) (to arrange) a time when we (to can meet) (to discuss) this matter in detail.

20. A multinational recently (to acquire) the company while the company (to undergo) still major re-engineering. The acquisition (to cause) six key members of staff (to defect) to rival companies. Three other key members (to indicate) that they (to leave) in the near future.

---

21. The company (to see) a significant increase in production over the last year but as we (to look) to the coming year, we (to expect) the increase (to fall) slightly. We (to develop) a new strategy in the last two months and we (to implement) this strategy in the first quarter next year.

---

22. We (to put) always the quality of our production first but in future we (to think) also of marketing more aggressively. We (to hope) (to increase) our sales potential this way. We (to work) with the new agency for at least a year before we (to see) a measurable difference in our sales.

---

23. The trader (to invest) in an international company without the prior permission of the board. As a result, we (to not be able) (to recover) the money after the company (to collapse). We (to need) (to establish) clear procedures which (to prevent) this from happening in future although the amount of money (to be) small.

---

24. The company's two new products (to enter) production next month and we (to expect) (to be) in the marketplace before the end of the year. Nevertheless, we (to can not stress) enough the importance of continuing (to promote) our existing production line. Furthermore, we (to need) (to conduct) this promotion with the same amount of vigour as we (to have) in the past.

(For answers see pages 181–187)

2.5 **Subject and verb agreement**

The function of subject and verb agreement

A relationship exists between the subject and the main verb of a sentence. The main verb must agree with the subject of the sentence in *person* and *number* (see also Nouns, Verbs, and Sentences). Consequently, we cannot put a *plural* main verb with a *singular* subject and neither can we put a *singular* main verb with a *plural* subject.

Instead, we must put a *plural* main verb with a *plural* subject and we must put a *singular* main verb with a *singular* subject. In each case, we always agree the main verb to the subject.

Basic verb conjugation

I have conjugated below the auxiliary verb *to be* in the simple tense.

Person	Past	Present	Future
I	was	am	will be
You	were	are	will be
He/she/it	was	is	will be
We	were	are	will be
You	were	are	will be
They	were	are	will be

I have conjugated below the auxiliary verb *to do* in the simple tense.

Person	Past	Present	Future
I	did	do	will do
You	did	do	will do
He/she/it	did	does	will do
We	did	do	will do
You	did	do	will do
They	did	do	will do

I have conjugated below the auxiliary verb *to have* in the simple tense.

Person	Past	Present	Future
I	had	have	will have
You	had	have	will have
He/she/it	had	has	will have
We	had	have	will have
You	had	have	will have
They	had	have	will have

Collective nouns

We use collective nouns to identify groups of people or things. Collective nouns are all *singular* so collective nouns should take always a *singular* verb (see also Nouns).
The team is; management is; the council is; and staff is.

Countable nouns

We can form countable nouns into *plurals*. A plural noun makes a plural subject and a plural subject takes a plural verb (see also Nouns).
Four people are; ten chairs are; and the members are.

Uncountable nouns

We cannot count uncountable nouns and so we cannot form uncountable nouns into *plurals*. We think of uncountable nouns as *singular* in subject and verb agreement even though uncountable nouns have no number (see also Nouns).
The air is; the weather is; and money is.

Singular expressions

Some expressions appear to be *plural* but are always *singular*. We call these expressions singular expressions. I have listed the singular expressions below.

none	nobody	either one
anyone	each	anybody
neither one	either	someone
no one	somebody	neither
everyone	each one	everybody

Furthermore, we should use always a singular pronoun with a singular expression (see also Pronouns).
Everyone must clear his or her shelf by next week.

Compound subjects

Sometimes we join more than one subject together to form what we call a compound subject. Two or more subjects joined by the conjunction *and* form *one plural* subject.
John and Nowida (compound subject) **are leading** (plural main verb) *the team*.

Some compound subjects involve *a choice* between one of the subjects. *Either/or* and *neither/nor* means *one or the other*. Compound subjects which involve a choice can be either singular or plural depending on the original subject.
Neither the listener (singular subject) *nor the speaker* (singular subject) *is* (singular main verb) *at fault*.
Neither skateboarders (plural subject) *nor rollerskaters* (plural subject) *are* (plural main verb) *allowed in the park*.

Sometimes we have a choice between a singular subject and a plural subject. In these cases, the main verb should agree with the subject to which the main verb is *closest in position*.
Either Jani (singular subject) *or David and Kim* (plural subject) *are* (plural main verb) *responsible for the launch*.
Neither the cleaners (plural subject) *nor their manager* (singular subject) *is* (singular main verb) *attending the briefing*.

Academic subjects, measurements, and units

We think of academic subjects, measurements, and units as *singular*. We refer to academic subjects as singular because we have abbreviated academic subjects from their original form such as *the humanities' department*.
Humanities is.
Forty miles is.
Two-hundred-and-fifty pounds is (see also Compound Adjectives and Numerals).

Agreement and the passive voice

We are more likely to make subject and verb agreement mistakes in the passive voice. The passive voice emphasises the object of a sentence over the subject (see also Sentences). The order of a passive voice sentence is object, main verb, and possibly subject (see also Active and Passive Voice).
Staff (object) **are expected** (passive main verb) *to complete the questionnaire*.
We (subject) **expect** (active main verb) *staff* (object) *to complete the questionnaire*.

Notice that in the passive voice we agree the main verb to the object of the sentence and not to the subject.

Writing tips for subject and verb agreement

Keep the subject and the main verb of the sentence together to make fewer subject and verb agreement mistakes. Furthermore, write in the active voice to make fewer subject and verb agreement mistakes (see also Active and Passive Voice). Finally, put the subject and verb *first* in the sentence since the subject and the main verb are the message of the sentence.

Use personal pronouns to make fewer mistakes with subject and verb agreement (see also Pronouns).
We (plural subject) *have decided* (plural main verb) *to change the policy.*

Writing *staff **is*** is strictly correct since *staff* is a collective noun and so staff is *singular*. Change the subject to a plural form if in doubt.
Staff members (plural subject) ***are*** (plural main verb) *free to decide for themselves.*

Use a singular pronoun with a singular expression. Alternatively, make the subject of the sentence plural.
Everyone must clear **his or her** *shelf by next week.*
Team members must clear **their** *shelves by next week.*

Subject and verb agreement exercises

Essential exercises

Consider the agreement between the subject and the main verb in the following sentences. Rewrite the sentences if the subject and the main verb disagree. In each case, change the main verb to agree with the subject.

1. The team are meeting next week.

   _____

2. The council meet today in Room 509.

   _____

3. The media is discussing a new policy.

   _____

4. The premises closes at 9.00pm on weeknights.

   _____

5. The data are stored on the hard drive of the computer.

   _____

6. Staff is responsible for the maintenance of the storeroom.

7. We sent a memo explaining how the department are accountable for the new policy.

_____

8. The support staff feels that management do not communicate everything which support staff need to know.

Bridging exercises Consider the agreement between the subject and the main verb in the following sentences. Rewrite the sentences if the subject and the main verb disagree. In each case, change the main verb to agree with the subject.

9. We introduced a policy of continuous maintenance in the department a year ago. Consequently, everyone of us now are doing his or her share.

_____

10. The new system saves time and money for the department. As a result, none of us have the right of not participating since we all benefit from the new system.

_____

11. The department meeting takes place on Wednesday at 10.30am. Either Sunil or Mary are presenting the team's monthly report. A copy of the report will be available tomorrow.

_____

12. A number of changes have occurred in the section since the merger. Many people have seen their jobs alter and management have to create the structures to facilitate these changes.

_____

13. A series of thefts have occurred in the building and a number of laptops have gone missing. However, neither management nor the relevant consultants feels that an independent investigation is necessary.

_____

14. The Board of Directors are meeting in London on Thursday morning. Consequently, the conference rooms on the third floor will be unavailable. Furthermore, the Directors are going to have lunch on the terrace from 12.00pm.

15. We are expanding our client base as part of our new drive to increase our profit margin. The team have compiled a proposal which will outline our new strategy. Either Patricia, the team leader, or the consulting team are presenting the new document.

---

16. The main objectives of the quarterly report is to outline the key changes. We need to implement these changes to the production process to improve both speed and quality. However, none of the report's three recommendations are suitable for our purposes.

Applied exercises Consider the agreement between the subject and the main verb in the following sentences. Rewrite the sentences if the subject and the main verb disagree. In each case, change the main verb to agree with the subject.

17. A large portion of the profits have disappeared as a result of our new staff recruitment. The recruitment of new staff members mean that our overheads have risen without us generating new income. The appendices contains a full breakdown on the cost of recruitment.

---

18. The media has leaked information contained in a report which the company have not published yet. Senior management meet this afternoon to discuss the legal implications of the leak. The agenda covers a discussion on whether or not the media is legally responsible for the leak.

---

19. The group have decided to change the focus of the project. Initially, the project focused on the marketing plan for the company's two new products. However, the Senior Management Team have decided to delay the launch of both products. Consequently, the group do not have a specific project on which to focus at the moment.

20. The first floor have to evacuate the building by taking the following route. Staff must descend by the rear stairway and exit through the rear entrance. Furthermore, the second floor have to evacuate the building in a similar fashion. However, the third floor have to descend the front stairway and exit the building through the main entrance.

21. Twenty-five per cent of profits have fallen in the last quarter. The finance department have compiled a report which outlines the speculation over the sudden decrease. Nevertheless, the report also indicates that 10% of costs also have fallen. Consequently, the fall in profits are not as threatening as the initial figures in the report suggests.

22. The budget of the marketing team have escalated in the last six months. Consequently, the profit margin of the team have lessened proportionately. Management are concerned about the situation and about where the budget may go in future. As a result, management have asked the team to provide suggestions to reduce the costs of production.

23. The department have cancelled the three-day workshop for catering staff. Four members of the human resources department arranged the workshop to help catering staff. The main objectives of the workshop was to develop new systems of communication for internal customers. However, the demands of the autumn season on the kitchen means that none of the staff are available to attend.

24. The key goals of the Financial Support Team is outlined in the new systems proposal. The department expect all members of the team to attend a briefing on the new document by the end of the month. Furthermore, the department invite members of the team to submit their questions or objections before the briefing. The department are preparing currently a questionnaire to circulate to the team.

(For answers see pages 188–192)

2.6 **Active and passive voice**

The function of active and passive voice

We have established already that a sentence must have a subject and a main verb to be complete (see also Sentences). Furthermore, we have established that the sentence can have also an object if the main verb is a transitive verb.

We use voice to write about either the subject of a sentence in relation to the main verb or the object of a sentence in relation to the main verb. We can place the *emphasis* on either the subject noun or the object noun by changing their *positions* in the sentence. We change the main verb accordingly when we change the position of the subject, the main verb, and the object.

We can change the *position* of the subject and the object in a sentence but we cannot change the *function* of the subject or the object. The subject of a sentence is always the noun which *performs* the action of the main verb of the sentence. Similarly, the object of a sentence is always the noun which *receives* the action of the main verb of the sentence. The main verb of a sentence is the verb which identifies both an *action* and a *tense*. The tense indicates *when* an action took place (see also Nouns, Verbs and Tense).

Identifying the subject and the main verb

We can use the following questions to identify the subject and verb in these sentences.

Many people use the computers.

Who does the action?	*Many people.*
What action do the people do?	They *use.*
In what tense is this sentence?	The present tense.
When do the people perform the action?	They *use* all the time.
Who or what receives the action?	*The computers.*

The computers are used by many people.

Who does the action?	*Many people.*
What action do the people do?	They *use.*
In what tense is this sentence?	The present tense.
When do the people perform the action?	They *use* all the time.
Who or what receives the action?	*The computers.*

The *information* in these two sentences is the same but the *emphasis* is different. The first sentence emphasises the people while the second sentence emphasises the computers.

The structure of the active and passive voice

The order of an active sentence is subject, main verb, and object.
Many people (subject) *use* (active main verb) *the computers* (object).

The order of a passive sentence is object, main verb, and (possibly) subject.
The computers (object) *are used* (passive main verb) [*by many people* (subject)].

We conjugate or form passive verbs by using: the auxiliary verb *to be*; the infinitive verb without the preposition *to*; and the passive participle *-en*, *-ne*, or *–ed* (see also Verbs). The auxiliary verb *to be* carries the tense of the verb (see also Tense).
To be plus **instruct** plus **–ed** equals **to be instructed**.

We can choose whether or not to include the subject in a passive sentence. We introduce the subject with the word *by*. Remember that the subject of a sentence is still always the person or thing which *performs* the action of the main verb. Nevertheless, we place the object before the main verb in a passive sentence. Furthermore, we agree the main verb to the object of the sentence in the passive voice (see also Subject and Verb Agreement).

Writing tips for active and passive voice

Use the active voice. Use the passive voice only where appropriate. For example, use the passive voice when you do not know who performed an action. Alternatively, use the passive voice when the object is more important than the subject in the mind of the user.

Put the subject and main verb in the first position in the sentence. Keep the subject and main verb together. Separating the subject and main verb with extra information makes the subject and main verb difficult to identify.

Be aware of how voice influences your style and tone. Be equally aware of how voice influences the way in which you think.

Active and passive voice exercises

Essential exercises

Change the following sentences into the active voice if the sentences are in the passive voice. Leave the sentences unchanged if the sentences are in the active voice.

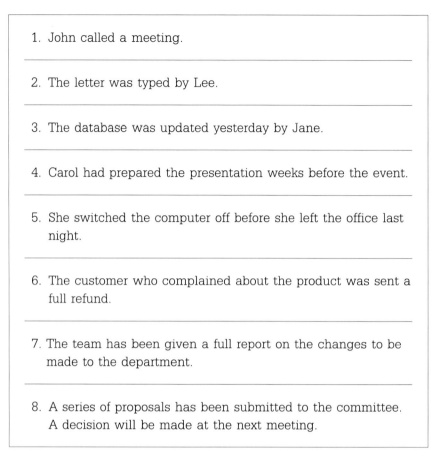

1. John called a meeting.

2. The letter was typed by Lee.

3. The database was updated yesterday by Jane.

4. Carol had prepared the presentation weeks before the event.

5. She switched the computer off before she left the office last night.

6. The customer who complained about the product was sent a full refund.

7. The team has been given a full report on the changes to be made to the department.

8. A series of proposals has been submitted to the committee. A decision will be made at the next meeting.

Bridging exercises   Change the following sentences into the active voice if the sentences are in the passive voice. Leave the sentences unchanged if the sentences are in the active voice.

9. The post was delivered this morning to reception. However, the package which we were expecting had not been sent with the delivery.

10. The room will be cleaned when we leave. Nevertheless, those attending the seminar are expected to clear any waste before leaving.

11. We were met at the reception and taken upstairs. However, we were left to wait in a small room without refreshments for nearly half-an-hour.

12. He reported the mistake but nothing was done. As a result, an investigation into the system is awaited and a full report has been commissioned.

13. Rachel was unhappy about the way Martin had spoken to her at the meeting. Nevertheless, an agreement was made to finish the project together.

14. The supplies have been delivered consistently behind schedule in the last month. Furthermore, the quality of the products has not been to standard.

15. The structure of the book has been reworked extensively since the first draft. However, no clearance has been given for the publication of the material.

16. The costs have been calculated and approval for the project is being sought currently. Approval for the figures is expected from the committee by the end of the month.

Applied exercises Change the following sentences into the active voice if the sentences are in the passive voice. Leave the sentences unchanged if the sentences are in the active voice.

17. No applications will be considered by the Board from now on unless those applications are submitted in writing before the end of the year.

18. The computers must be kept clear of all food and drink. In the past, the equipment has been damaged due to carelessness and indifference.

19 Fortunately, the figures for January show an increase in income; however, the figures show also a proportionate increase in expenses so we have no measurable difference in profits.

20. The workload is expected to increase in the coming months. Consequently, members of the team will have to alternate shifts in order to manage the new pressures in a way which best suits our needs.

---

21. Profits have been inflated in the last quarter due to the recent merger. A full report has been compiled and the Board has been briefed on the implications. However, no new developments are anticipated in the coming months.

---

22. The current change in administration has created two new positions which will have to be filled before the end of June. Production is needed urgently to run efficiently as the system has been scheduled for redesign next year. Consequently further delays are expected.

---

23. The measurements have been taken on your house. Nevertheless, the new landing will not be able to be installed until the carpet is removed completely from the lounge area below. Damage has been incurred in the past and removal will prevent that damage from happening again.

---

24. The construction of the warehouse has been completed. The arrival of stock is expected to begin in the next few weeks according to the instructions of the company. However, the company is warned that until the roof has been checked completely, no guarantees can be given as to the safety of the warehouse.

(For answers see pages 193–200)

2.7 **Modals and conditionals**

The function and type of modal verbs

We use modal verbs to *modify* or *change* the main verb of a sentence. Modal verbs allow us to write about *certainty, possibility, intention, obligation*, and *permission*. We use modal verbs with an infinitive verb without the preposition *to*. We would not know normally that the verb was infinitive but we can see the presence of the infinitive verb immediately with the verb *to be*.

*We **might go** into a new market.*

*You **could be** in a position to change the structure.*

Modal verbs include *can, could, able to, may, might, will, would, shall, should, must* and *ought to*.

The meaning of modal verbs

Can, could, and able to

We use *can*, *could*, and *able to* when something we want to do is *possible*. The action is possible either because we are physically able to do the action or because circumstances will make the action possible.

*Sima **can** speak four languages.*

*The team **could** have either individual targets or a team target.*

*You will be **able to** use the new system after hours.*

We use *could* both as the past tense of *can* and as a modal verb in its own right to indicate *possibility*.

*We **could have chosen** a different model* (past tense).

*I **could offer** you an alternative instead* (modal verb).

May and might

We use *may* for *permission* and *possibility*. We also use *might* for *possibility*. Furthermore, we use *might* as the past tense of *may* in indirect speech (see also Direct and Indirect Speech).

*You **may use** the machine for office work only* (permission).

*We **might decide** to update the programme this year* (possibility).

Will, would, and shall

We use *will* to form the future tenses. We also use *will* to write about things which we *intend* to do. In this case, we can use *will* for *emphasis*.

*The committee **will review** the procedure* (intention).
*We **will finish** the project by the end of the month* (emphasis).

We use **would** as the past tense of **will**.
*The director **would have been** here but he has been delayed* (past tense).

We use **shall** to mean the same as **will**. In other words, we use **shall** to write about *intention*. We used **shall** as a modal verb more often in the past but we use **shall** less often now. We tend to use **will** instead. We also use **shall** to show *obligation*.
*We **shall** be in production by the beginning of the year* (intention).
*You **shall** put the equipment away* (obligation).

Should and ought to

We use **should** and **ought to** to write about actions which our conscience, our intuition, or our acumen tell us to do but for some reason we do not. We also use **should** to write about things which we *expect* to happen.
*The company **should** invest more widely* (acumen).
*The business **ought to** sell some of its stock* (acumen).
*The report **should** arrive on Friday* (expectation).

Must

We use **must** to write about actions which are *obligatory*. In other words, we have no choice but to perform these actions. Consequently, we use **must** for procedures and regulations. However, we can use the imperative mood to achieve the same effect. We use the imperative mood to give commands or instructions. We do not use a subject in this mood because the subject is the user (see also Sentences).
*You **must** throw the gloves away after you have used them* (modal verb).
Throw the gloves away after you have used them (imperative mood).

The function of conditional sentences

We use conditional sentences to write about actions which will happen only if certain conditions are in place. These actions and conditions can be either *real* or these actions and conditions can be *unreal* or *hypothetical*.

The type and meaning of conditional sentences

We have four main types of conditional sentences. We use the first two types to write about *real* situations; and we use the second two types to write about *unreal or hypothetical* situations. However, we need to be aware that some grammarians identify more than four types of conditional sentences.

The conditional sentences which I have chosen to write about are all made of two clauses. These conditional sentences have an *action clause* and a *condition clause* (see also Phrases and Clauses). The two clauses are always joined by the conjunction *if* (see also Conjunctions).

The zero conditional
We use the zero conditional to write about situations which are likely to be true. Consequently, we use the present simple tense in both clauses. We use the present simple tense for situations which are always true (see Tense). The zero conditional structure is useful for *procedures* and *instructions*.
Switch *the machine off if the red light* **comes on**.

The first conditional
We use the first conditional to write about actions which we *intend* to perform in future if the conditions are right. Consequently, we use the future simple tense in the action clause and the present tense in the condition clause.
We **will buy** *the stock if the price* **falls**.

The second conditional
We use the second conditional to write about hypothetical situations. Consequently, we use the present simple tense and the modal verbs *would*, *could*, and *might* in the action clause. Furthermore, we use the past simple tense in the condition clause.
We **could receive** *benefits if we* **joined** *the scheme*.

The third conditional
We use the third conditional to write about hypothetical situations which should have happened in the past. Consequently, we use the present perfect tense and the modal verbs *would*, *should*, and *could have* with the past participle in the action clause. Furthermore, we use the past perfect tense in the condition clause.
We **would have sold** *our shares if the index prices* **had risen**.

Writing tips for conditional sentences
We used to consider starting a sentence with a conjunction as grammatically incorrect. Now we consider starting a sentence with a conjunction in formal business writing as an *inappropriate* style (see also Conjunctions).

Avoid starting a sentence with a conjunction by switching the two clauses of a conditional sentence. You will start your sentences with a clear subject and main verb also if you switch the action clause with the condition clause (see also Conjunctions).

Write *if the machine stops, push the red button* as *push the red button if the machine stops*.
(See also Imperative Mood).

2.8 **Direct and indirect speech**

The function of direct speech

We use direct speech to *quote* the exact words which someone has said in the past. Consequently, we use quotation marks whenever we use direct speech (see also Punctuation). Direct speech is particularly relevant in legal documents, appraisals, disciplinary hearings, business journalism, and the minutes of some meetings.
Lorraine said: "I will not be able to attend on Thursday".

The punctuation of direct speech

We use quotation marks when we quote complete sentences and when we quote phrases or clauses. Furthermore, we introduce a quotation with a colon (see also Punctuation). Some companies use single quotation marks as their house style for quoting single words or phrases. We also can use quotation marks for controversial words or for words whose meaning we question.
*The department suggested that we reconsider our approach to "**Third World**" markets.*

Speech verbs

We use speech verbs to write about *what* other people said or about *how* those people said something. We also call speech verbs *reporting verbs*. We always use speech verbs in the past tense (see also Tense). Speech verbs include *to say; to ask; to answer; to question; to reply;* and *to state* (see also Verbs). We use speech verbs in both direct and indirect speech.

The function of indirect speech

We use indirect speech to *report* the words which someone has said in the past. We also call indirect speech *reported speech* for this reason. Consequently, we use no quotation marks in indirect speech.
The participants said that they enjoyed the conference.

Changes in determiners and references in indirect speech

We change the *determiners* and *references* when we report someone's words in indirect speech (see also Articles and Determiners).
This becomes *that*.
Here becomes *there*.
Now becomes *then*.

Changes in time references in indirect speech

We change the *time references* when we report someone's words in indirect speech.
Today becomes *that day*.
Yesterday becomes *the previous day*.
Tomorrow becomes *the following day*.
This week/month/year becomes *that week/month/year*.
Last week/month/year becomes *the previous week/month/year*.
Next week/month/year becomes *the following week/month/year*.

Changes in modal verbs in indirect speech

We change the modal verb of the sentence when we report someone's words in indirect speech (see also Modal Verbs).
Will becomes *would*.
Can become *could*.
May becomes *might*.

Changes in tense in indirect speech

We change the tense of the main verb when we report someone's words in indirect speech. All tenses take one step back. In all future tenses, the modal verb *will* becomes *would* (see Changes in Modal Verbs in Indirect Speech above).
The present simple becomes *the past simple*.
The present continuous becomes *the past continuous*.
The present perfect becomes *the past perfect*.
The present perfect continuous becomes *the past perfect continuous*.
The past perfect stays *the past perfect*.

The use of *that* in indirect speech

We can write indirect speech with or without the relative pronoun *that* (see also Relative Pronouns). We create a more formal tone in our writing when we use the relative pronoun *that*. Conversely, we create a more informal tone in our writing when we omit the relative pronoun *that* (see also Style and Tone).
*Gautam said **that** he would arrange the meeting* (formal).
Gautam said he would arrange the meeting (informal).

Direct and indirect speech exercises

Essential exercises

Change the following transcripts into indirect speech.

1. Samantha: I agree.

_____

2. Peter: I'm sorry I'm late.

_____

3. Tony: What do you think, Julia?

4. Leigh: And our customers are complaining about our forms.

---

5. Colin: Do you realise how the committee will respond when they hear?

---

6. Franco: I felt the group did not listen to my point of view because people were trying to meet their own needs.

Bridging exercises Change the following transcripts into indirect speech.

7. Officer: You say the accident happened at two 'o clock in the morning. Why didn't anybody call the police straight away?

---

8. Mark: Can you leave your questions until I've finished the presentation. I find interruptions distracting and then I forget key pieces of information.

---

9. Chairperson: We will meet again next week if everyone is free on Monday. Can everyone attend on that day? Good, I'll circulate the agenda this Friday.

---

10. She: What we have seen here today shows how effectively the team has worked in the last six months. We have seen a 15% increase in profits and a 5% decrease in cost.

---

11. He: We had four comments that were particularly interesting. Shall I list them for you? The venue is too small; the lunch was inadequate; the room had no air conditioning; and the presentation was too long.

---

12. Barbara: The truck rolled on the highway at four o' clock this morning. No one was killed in the accident. However, the driver was badly injured and is now in intensive care. The co-driver was unhurt but is in a state of shock.

Change the following transcripts into indirect speech.

13. Jennifer: Mike, did you have any new ideas about the project over the weekend? Last week, you seemed particularly inspired about the work. In fact, I thought that some of the ideas you had would work brilliantly. Would you like to share those ideas with the group?

14. Reshna: We need to need to change the culture of the organisation if we are going to see any long-term results. We will achieve little if we ask people to behave differently without giving those people the opportunity to change in the workplace. We'll be sending a mixed message to the staff.

15. Richard: Over the next few months we will see a steady increase in costs as we take on more staff who will be inducted first before starting work about three months from now. We need everyone to be clear that the increase is a short-term effect. In fact, we expect to see an increase in production when the new staff have found their feet.

16. Anne: We're not really sure yet how to put it all into place. We've thought of asking managers to check that people have completed the self-assessment during their one-to-ones but that, of course, puts an extra burden on the managers who have enough to do as it is. We were hoping to get some more ideas from the group. Does anyone have any suggestions?

17. Jousef: But our service users expect more attention now. We have to consider what they want first before we make any changes to our services. We can't just go ahead and make decisions without asking the people we're supposed to be helping first. I suggest that we either set up a focus group to find out what our users want or we put together a questionnaire to find out people's views.

18. Henry: I want to – um – begin by – well, you all know each other, don't you. Don't you? Good. That's what I thought. Anyway, – um – let's get started then. Welcome everyone to the – ah – to our meeting. The – ah – first item is John (laughter). No, I mean – well, you know what I mean (more laughter). John is, of course, presenting the first item. You are presenting the first item, aren't you John? Good. Over to you, John.

(For answers see pages 200–202)

2.9 **Review**

Forming words into groups

We looked in Part Two at how we form words into groups. We looked firstly at phrases and clauses and we identified what makes a phrase or a clause different from a sentence.

The components of a sentence

Then we looked at sentences and we identified that sentences need at least a subject and a main verb to be complete. We also saw that some sentences can take an object if the main verb of the sentence is transitive. The sentence will have usually a predicative adjective if the main verb is intransitive.

The types of sentences

We also looked at the types of sentences and we saw that sentences can be simple, compound, or complex. A simple sentence has at least a subject and a main verb and possibly an object or a predicative adjective. A compound sentence is two or more simple sentences joined by a conjunction such as *and*. Finally, a complex sentence can be either a simple sentence or a compound sentence containing one or more clauses.

The types of tense

We examined the types of tenses and when and how we form these tenses. The three main tenses in English are the past, present, and future tenses. We can divide the tenses further into the simple, continuous, and perfect tenses.

We use the simple tense to write about events *which happen and finish*. We use the continuous tense to write about events *which are in progress at a particular point in time*. Finally, we use the perfect tenses to write *about more than one event in the past or future*; and to write about events *which begin in the past and which are relevant to the present*.

Subject and verb agreement

We established after tense that the subject and the main verb of a sentence must agree in *person* and *number*. We call this rule subject and verb agreement. We saw that we are most likely to make subject and verb agreement errors with compound subjects; collective nouns; singular expressions; *choices* between more than one subject; and the passive voice. We saw that in the passive voice we agree the main verb in number to the *object* of the sentence. Consequently, we break the fundamental rule of subject and verb agreement in the passive voice.

Active and passive voice

We looked at the active and passive voice after subject and verb agreement. Here we saw that we can change the *order* of the subject, the main verb, and the object of a sentence. We emphasise the subject of the sentence in the active voice. We emphasise the object of a sentence in the passive voice and we change the main verb accordingly. In other words, we put the object in front of the main verb and we agree the two in number in the passive voice. Active and passive voice is a style choice which will affect the tone of our writing.

Modal verbs and conditional sentences

We continued by looking at modal verbs which allow us to write about *possibility*, *certainty*, *intention*, *obligation*, and *permission*. We looked at conditional sentences in relation to modal verbs and we saw that conditional sentences allow us to write about *real* or *hypothetical* situations. Conditional sentences are relevant to people who write *procedures*, *instructions*, and *specifications*.

Direct and indirect speech

Finally, we looked at direct and indirect speech which allow us to write about the things which other people say. Direct and indirect speech forms are useful for people who take and write *minutes* and for people who write *press releases*.

Structuring sentences into paragraphs

Now we are going to look at how we structure sentences into paragraphs. We will look at what happens *within* a paragraph and what happens *between* paragraphs. We will see also how we make sense of information through the use of punctuation. Finally, we will explore how we make our message acceptable through our use of style and tone.

PART THREE

Structuring information

3.1 **Preview**

Words, sentences, and paragraphs

We looked in Parts One and Two at the types of words which we use and how we form those words into different types of sentences. Now we are going to look at how we form sentences into paragraphs and at how we organise paragraphs with punctuation.

Characteristics of paragraphs

We will explore the topic sentence of each paragraph and how we can develop the topic sentence. We will look also at the length of paragraphs and their layout. More importantly, we will look at how we bind paragraphs both *within* paragraphs and *between* paragraphs. We call this quality of unity in writing *cohesion and coherence*.

Punctuation and style and tone

We will look at punctuation after cohesion and coherence. We use punctuation to *guide* our users through our information. We will look also at what constitutes style and tone and at how style and tone affect our business writing.

The final self-assessment

Style and tone will bring us to the end of our exploration of grammar. However, another self-assessment will be waiting for you in the Appendices to assess how much you have learnt through using The Workbook.

3.2 **Paragraphs**

The function of paragraphs

We use paragraphs to break information into units. Units of information are more manageable for both the writer and the user. We use a new paragraph *for every new topic*. In other words, we should use a new paragraph every time we change direction in our thinking or even when we look at an idea from a new angle.

Cohesion and coherence

We use paragraphs to make sense of information and to create unity in a text. We create unity in a text by creating cohesion and coherence. Cohesion and coherence are difficult to separate. In other words, cohesion and coherence are two sides of the same coin like style and tone (see also Style and Tone). Furthermore, cohesion and coherence tend to create each other.

We use cohesion to *bind* a paragraph. Furthermore, we use cohesion to bind *groups* of paragraphs. Consequently, we can say that we also use cohesion to bind sections, chapters, and texts in general.

We use coherence to make paragraphs and texts *understandable*. We use typical *patterns* of structuring information to make the paragraph or text understandable to our user. Users expect these patterns even if users are unaware of these patterns. In other words, users have internalised these patterns subconsciously. Users are unlikely to be able to make sense of a text without effort if the patterns are absent.

Ways to create cohesion and coherence

We can use *topic sentences*; *keywords*; *linking words*; *paragraphs*; *subheadings*; *the techniques of exposition*; *chapter headings*; *glossaries*; *formal structure*; *introductions*; *conclusions*; *summaries*; and *recommendations* to create cohesion and coherence in business writing.

The use of topic sentences

Each paragraph which we write should have a topic sentence. The topic sentence tells the user about what we are writing in the paragraph. The topic sentence is usually the first sentence in the paragraph.

Sometimes, we cannot have a topic sentence in each paragraph especially in short letters or memos. However, topic sentences make reading easier in long texts such as reports. Topic sentences allow the user to skim or speed read the text and still understand the main point of the writing. Users often read the topic sentences only of each paragraph when users skim read a text. The topic sentences alone should give the user a clear overview of the whole text.

The use of keywords

We use keywords to bind the sentences in a paragraph. Consequently, we also use keywords to bind groups of paragraphs into sections, chapters, and texts as a whole.

Synonyms are *different words with the same meaning* such as *prison* and *jail*. We should be aware of using too many synonyms in business writing because synonyms can make skimming or speed reading our text difficult for the user. Instead, we should establish keywords initially in a text and then use those keywords throughout the text.

The use of linking words

We use linking words to join sentences in a paragraph. We also use linking words to join paragraphs in a text. Most linking words are conjunctive adverbs. However, some linking words are linking phrases and these phrases are usually conjunctive phrases. Linking words show the user how the ideas in the text fit. I have included a comprehensive list of linking words in *the parts of speech* (see Conjunctions).

The length of paragraphs

Paragraphs are as long as paragraphs need to be in order to discuss a topic. However, one guideline we can use is to limit our paragraphs to between *three and six* sentences. Shorter paragraphs are easier to read and are more inviting to the user. We should break our paragraphs into smaller units if our paragraphs are too long. Furthermore, we should rewrite our topic sentences accordingly.

The number and layout of paragraphs

We should have at least three paragraphs per page although more would be better. Shorter, well-spaced paragraphs are easier to read and more inviting to the user.

We should block our paragraphs to the left and leave a single line space between each paragraph. An open layout is easier to read and more inviting to the user.

We should avoid fully justifying our paragraphs since a fully-justified paragraph is difficult to proofread. Instead, we should left-justify our paragraphs and leave the right margin unjustified.

The use of
subheadings

We should use as many subheadings as we can in business writing. Primarily, subheadings help the user to focus on the key points in the text. Subheadings also help the user to find key pieces of information quickly. Furthermore, subheadings help a user to speed read a text with ease. Finally, efficient users will reread the subheadings only to summarise the main points of the text.

One guideline to good writing practice is to create our subheadings *after* we have finished writing the main body of the text. Consequently, our subheadings will reflect clearly the key points which we have made in our text.

The techniques
of exposition

We should focus on *facts*, *actions*, *suggestions*, *decisions*, and *time-scales* in our business writing. We can use *example*; *analogy*; *classification*; *definition*; *explanation*; *cause and effect*; *comparison and contrast*; and *process analysis* to support our main point. We should express our main points clearly in our topic sentences (see also Topic Sentences). We can create focus in our writing by omitting any details which do not contribute to our objectives. All details should contribute to our user accepting our message so that we can achieve our purpose (see also Style and Tone).

**Writing tips
for
paragraphs**

Use a topic sentence for each paragraph in longer documents.

Be consistent in your use of keywords even if you feel that you are repeating yourself. Too many synonyms can make speed reading your text difficult for your user.

Keep your paragraphs to between three and six sentences. Have at least three paragraphs per page. Block your paragraphs and leave a space between each paragraph. Only left-justify your paragraphs.

Use subheadings throughout your text.

Paragraph exercises

Essential exercise

Divide the following text into paragraphs. Remember that each paragraph should begin with a topic sentence. Remember also that no paragraph should explore more than one topic.

Start by finding and underlining the topic sentences. Topic sentences often contain linking words but never assume that a sentence with a linking word is a topic sentence. Always test the topic sentence. The sentences which follow the topic sentence should develop the topic in some way. Sentences which go in a new direction indicate a new topic.

We currently are introducing an expensive new telephone system into the company. After long discussion, we decided to buy the new system despite the initial extra cost. We made this decision by establishing a telephone committee which we created last year. The committee has been meeting once a month to evaluate our situation and to establish our needs as a business. The new telephone system will cost the company over £200,000. However, we expect the system to start paying for itself by the end of the year. We need the new system because the system will benefit our business in a number of ways. Primarily, the old telephone system slowed the speed of our response to clients. Moreover, we often cut clients off or put clients on hold. Furthermore, clients usually had to call back if they wanted another department. Finally, clients themselves had to call consultants who were teleworking from home. We will introduce the new telephone system into the company in October. Although we had hoped originally to have the new system in place by June, unforeseen circumstances stopped us from achieving our goal. Two events in particular took priority over installing the new system. Firstly, the basement flooded and the company had to claim over £100,000 in damages. Secondly, the Senior Management Team decided at the last minute to host an event at this year's Management Conference in London. We will introduce the new system gradually into the company. We will start firstly in the reception areas and then move systematically to the other floors of the building. We decided early in the planning to break the introduction of the new system into a series of stages. We made this decision for three reasons. Firstly, a graded introduction makes the process more manageable for both the staff and the committee. Secondly, a graded introduction makes the process faster. Finally, and perhaps most importantly, a graded introduction makes the process less expensive. The new system will cover eventually the entire company in all three of our bases in the city. We expect all members of staff at all levels in all three bases to be able to use the new system confidently. Consequently, we will train all staff members systematically before the end of September. Our goal is for everyone to be completely familiar with the new system by the time we put the system into operation in October. We will install a new telephone on every desk and in every room in the company. We also will install new phones in the homes of those members of staff who work from home more than twice a week. A cable company which operates throughout Europe will install and maintain the new system. We chose this company after exploring four other companies, two of which were national companies. The company we chose is only slightly less expensive and will take longer in fact to install the system than the other companies. However, we felt that the people with whom we worked listened to our needs; carefully considered our situation; put thought into their solution; and generally made us feel that they understood what we wanted.

Bridging exercise   Divide the following text into paragraphs. Remember that each paragraph should begin with a topic sentence. Remember also that no paragraph should explore more than one topic.

Start by finding and underlining the topic sentences. Topic sentences often contain linking words but never assume that a sentence with a linking word is a topic sentence. Always test the topic sentence. The sentences which follow the topic sentence should develop the topic in some way. Sentences which go in a new direction indicate a new topic.

Sales of the Captain Courage action figure have begun to drop steadily after a brilliant start to the financial year. Sales of the figure peaked in September this year at 60,000 units after a steady increase throughout the previous financial year. The September figures brought the overall sales of the action figure to half-a-million units since we launched the toy in November last year. However, the sales were down to 10,000 units by December this year. Independent studies show that record sales of the electronic game Traders helped to push the sales of the action figure down. The Marketing Team credited the initial success of the action figure to the popularity of the television show on which we based the toy. The show aired on national television at 6.00pm on Friday nights which research identified as an ideal time for the target audience. The show was number one on the ratings for the entire first season. Critics believe that the show's success was due to the appeal of leading actor Storm Majors. Majors is 6'2", has dark hair, blue eyes, and an athletic build. One critic described him as "the ideal combination of values and appearances". The action figure was low-cost because we manufactured the toy in Asia using a revolutionary new technique. Play Things Incorporated designed the action figure which is a combination of aluminium and silicone. The company is a leading Chicago-based toy designer. The action figure has a movable aluminium armature wrapped in a flexible silicone cover. We manufactured the figure in Asia because of the high level of quality and the low cost of production. We then transported the toy to our distribution centres around the world. Thirty per cent of the buyers were girls between the ages of nine and sixteen. Nevertheless, we had aimed the action figure primarily at boys between the ages of eight and fourteen. Bradford Consulting Agency provided us with an independent investigation which gave three reasons for the shift in the target market. Firstly, actor Storm Majors became popular unexpectedly and took part in a comprehensive publicity campaign to promote the show. Majors visited over 1,000 elementary schools during the show's first season. Observers commented on the actor's natural ease with children and his ability to give positive encouragement to both boys and girls. Secondly, the show created complex female characters which one feminist writer described as "empowered". The same writer went on to credit the success of the female characters to the fact that three of the show's five writers are women. Finally and most importantly, Captain Courage found a female side-kick half-way through the first season in the form of Rosa, a twelve year-old orphan girl. Sales of the action figure doubled three weeks after Rosa joined the show. The question which now remains is whether we should suspend the production line or whether we can adapt the line for a different use. Storm Majors' decision to follow a film career has threatened the future success of the television show. The show's producers are searching now for a replacement but no television show has replaced a lead actor successfully in the past. In the meantime, Ideas Unlimited has a new television show in development. The company has offered to license the characters to us provided that we use the same production technique as we do for Captain Courage. Ideas Unlimited is a Los Angeles-based independent production company. The producers plan to develop the new series into a full-length film.

Applied exercise Divide the following text into paragraphs. Remember that each paragraph should begin with a topic sentence. Remember also that no paragraph should explore more than one topic.

Start by finding and underlining the topic sentences. Topic sentences often contain linking words but never assume that a sentence with a linking word is a topic sentence. Always test the topic sentence. The sentences which follow the topic sentence should develop the topic in some way. Sentences which go in a new direction indicate a new topic.

The Retail and Private Clients Division (RPC) made a profit contribution of 40% to the overall results of the Bank. The RPC Division made the highest contribution and we attribute the increase to our decision to expand the Division's client base. In the past year, we focused more on self-employed and freelance clients and we also began to provide more financial services for small businesses. Furthermore, we increased the number of our high street branches to 1,500 which provided services to eight million clients. Finally, we focused our services on providing our clients with more personal finance products and portfolio investments. The Corporate and Institutional Banking Division (CIB) made a profit contribution of 32% to the overall results of the Bank. In this area, our client base remained National and Multinational Companies, Public Corporations, and Commercial Real Estate Clients. The CIB Division provided customer loans of 350 billion and managed deposits of 100 billion. We also increased the credit authorities of our 15,000 staff. Moreover, we expanded our Information Technology (IT) systems. Finally, we increased our consultancy services to support companies which are undergoing difficulties. In future, we plan to focus our services more clearly on the needs of our clients to ensure better returns and higher market shares. The Investment Banking Division (IB) made a profit contribution of 28% to the overall results of the Bank. The IB Division made the lowest contribution of the three income-earning groups. We attribute this low performance to poor results in the third quarter due to pressure in Asian financial markets. However, Emerging Markets increased business development and we also saw improvements in Structured Finance and Asset Management. Unfortunately, IB fell short of this year's targets. In future, we plan to focus more on our client's expectations of investment. Changes in the market mean that our clients expect comprehensive advice combined with efficient service. We plan to keep these areas together by integrating various parts of the Bank. We also plan to maximise our world-wide trading activities by increasing our market penetration and rearranging our internal structures to help us to meet our target levels. We have introduced a number of changes to increase the Bank's focus on the marketplace. We have increased our services primarily in IT and IT Operations (ITO) and in the function of our staff. We have increased significantly the electronic access that our clients have to the Bank. We aim to make banking attractive and easy for our clients. The developments which we have implemented are consistent and follow a strategic plan which the Operations Management Team (OMT) have designed. However, staff levels have been less consistent than growth at the Bank. We have to adjust the levels of our staff continually because of competition and technological changes in the workplace. We tend to keep staff whose jobs have a direct impact on our relationships with clients and we tend to cut staff in administrative roles. Furthermore, we decreased our domestic staff numbers by 10,000 last year while we increased our international staff numbers by 12,000. On the whole, our workforce dropped from 75,000 last year to 70,000 this year. These figures follow the employment trends of the last five years. Nevertheless, we put time and energy into developing systems for staff motivation in the Bank. We recognise that staff achievement is the foundation of the success of our business. We have placed the responsibility for human resources onto the Personnel Management Division (PMD). Staff motivation is inseparable from the development of our corporate identity and our policy of knowledge management. We see the allocation of personal responsibility to staff as a direct contribution to the achievement of our corporate targets. Last year, we introduced a remuneration policy which put our non-tariff staff onto a bonus system and we introduced a performance-related pay system. Furthermore, we invested 350 million in training and we created a part-time employment scheme for staff over 55. We found the part-time employment scheme more cost efficient than early retirement. The shares of the Bank increased significantly in the last reporting year. The market value of the shares rose and we saw an increase in value of nearly 75%. The increase in value was related to two factors. Firstly, the market expected consolidation in the global banking industry. Secondly, the market perceives the Bank to emerge as a front-runner in the EMU. The increase in value will improve also the long-term performance of the shares. The increase means that £10,000 worth of shares in 1980 were valued at nearly £85,000 at the end of last year provided that the investor had bought more shares. The total is almost twice the figure of the previous year and shows an average of a 10% annual return.

(For answers see pages 203–208)

3.3 **Punctuation**

The function of punctuation

We use punctuation to help our user to make sense of the information on the page. Good use of punctuation should make the information *easier* for the user to understand. Complicated punctuation can get in the way of good business communication (see also Style and Tone). We should use punctuation only when the punctuation will *contribute* to how the user makes sense of the information on the page.

Below is a list of the punctuation marks and how we use these marks. I have divided the list into groups to help you to understand how the punctuation marks *function*. The groups include *starting and finishing sentences*; *adding extra information*; *joining sentences, clauses, and phrases*; and *other punctuation marks*.

Starting and finishing sentences

Capital or upper case letters (A)

We use capital letters to *start* sentences so capital letters always follow a full stop, a question mark, or an exclamation mark. Americans use capital letters also after a colon.

We use capital letters for all proper nouns such as *London* throughout sentences (see also Nouns).

We never use capital letters in the middle of a word unless the word is a registered company or brand name such as *SmithKline Beecham*.

We use capital letters *after* quotation marks in direct speech (see also Direct and Indirect Speech).
Vicky said: "The report is in my office".

Full stops (.)

We use full stops to *end* sentences and we always follow full stops with capital letters. Americans call full stops *periods*.

We put full stops *outside* the quotation marks in direct speech (see also Direct and Indirect Speech).
Vicky said: "The report is in my office".

Question marks (?)

We use question marks to indicate that sentences are questions. Every question should end in a question mark.

We always use question marks at the *end* of questions only since question marks include full stops. Furthermore, we always follow question marks with capital letters since question marks always end sentences.

Exclamation marks (!)

We use exclamation marks to indicate that sentences are exclamations. In other words, we indicate that the sentence is dramatic or sensational. We also use exclamation marks at the end of interjections. I have chosen not to write about interjections in The Workbook because I feel that interjections have no place in business writing.

We always use exclamation marks at the *end* of exclamations only since exclamation marks include full stops. Furthermore, we always follow exclamation marks with capital letters since exclamation marks always end sentences.

Adding extra information

Commas (,)

We use commas in a list of adjectives which describes a noun.
*The presentation was **detailed, comprehensive and well-written**.*

We use commas to separate single-word items in a list.
*The report contains **a summary, recommendations, a glossary and an appendix**.*

Americans put a comma in front of the conjunction *and* in a single-word list of items. The British put no comma in front of the conjunction *and* in a single-word list of items. However, the British do put a comma in front of *and* when the final item is ambiguous or when the British consider the final item to be one thing.
*We offer soup, salad, **and bread and butter**.*

We use commas to divide phrases and subordinate clauses from the main clause of a sentence. We use two commas when identifying a relative clause or we use none at all. Commas are unnecessary in simple sentences. Instead, commas are more useful in complex sentences where the user will need more help in processing the information on the page (see also Phrases and Clauses).

We use commas for non-defining relative clauses (see also Relative Pronouns).
*The witness, **who refused to testify**, was unavailable for comment.*

We use commas to divide the clauses of a conditional sentence if we put the condition clause first (see also Conditional Sentences).

If you shut down the machine, reset the timer first.

We use commas after conjunctive adverbs both when the conjunctive adverb *starts* the sentence and when the conjunctive adverb *joins* two sentences.

The targets were remarkably high. **Nevertheless**, *the team achieved its goal.*

The targets were remarkably high; **nevertheless**, *the team achieved its goal.*

Parentheses
( )

We use parentheses or curved brackets to put *extra information* into a complete sentence. The extra information is usually *related but unessential* to the main point of the sentence. We consider parentheses to be stronger than commas. Consequently, we use parentheses for information which is an aside to the main point.

We put the full stop *outside* the parentheses when we add a phrase or clause to the *end* of a sentence. We always use parentheses in pairs. Using parentheses more than once per sentence or even per paragraph will overload the text with information.

We also use parentheses to add whole sentences of extra information to paragraphs. Whole sentences in parentheses in a paragraph function the same way which an extra clause or phrase functions in a sentence. We put the full stop *inside* the parentheses and we follow the parentheses with a capital letter if we add a whole sentence as extra information to a paragraph. The sentence would be an aside to the main topic of the paragraph but still related.

We use square brackets inside *direct quotations* to show that the writer has added the information. Parentheses are curved brackets which imply that the original speaker added the information as an aside. *(Sic)* means that the speaker made the mistake in the quotation and that the mistake is not a publishing error.

The dash
(–)

We use dashes to add extra information which is unessential to the main point of the sentence. Dashes function like commas and parentheses and so we always use dashes in pairs. We should use dashes only once per sentence and perhaps only once per paragraph.

We can include *explanations; amplifications; paraphrase; particular details;* and *corrections of preceding material* in both parentheses and dashes. However, putting extra information into a separate sentence will help to create clarity in our writing.

Joining sentences, clauses, and phrases

Semi-colons
(;)

We use semi-colons to *separate* phrases or clauses in a list (see also Phrases and Clauses).
We have three options: we could re-structure our management; we could merge with another company; or we could sell our share.

We use semi-colons to join *related but unconnected* sentences. Semi-colons suggest a *link* but semi-colons also keep the sentences *independent*. Using semi-colons in this way is a style choice (see also Style and Tone).
The team set high standards; everyone committed to achieving strenuous goals.

We use semi-colons before conjunctive adverbs when we use a conjunctive adverb to join two sentences.
The targets were remarkably high; **nevertheless**, *the team achieved its goal.*

Colons
(:)

We use colons to introduce both single-word lists and lists made of clauses, phrases, and sentences.
We have three options: we could re-structure our management; we could merge with another company; or we could sell our share.

We use colons to develop an idea which we introduce in the first part of a sentence. Sometimes we use the colon to introduce the *antithesis* of the idea in the first part of the sentence.
To err is human: to forgive is divine.

We use colons before a complete sentence which is in quotation marks. We use no colons before parts of sentences or single words which are in quotation marks.
Gemma said: "We need to consider alternative solutions to the problem".

Ampersands
(&)

We use ampersands to join two names when the names form the complete name of a company. We are required legally to use the ampersand if the company name is registered with an ampersand.
James & Jones.

We use the ampersand when we join three or more names and when two of those names form a unit.
Brown & Smith and Beeke wrote the screenplay.

We do not use the ampersand as a short form of the conjunction *and*. Instead, we write the conjunction *and* in full (see also Conjunctions).

**Quotation marks
(" ")**

We use quotation marks whenever we quote the exact words which someone has said in the past. Quotation marks are particularly relevant in legal documents; appraisals; disciplinary hearings; business journalism; press releases; and the minutes of some meetings. We use quotation marks for complete sentences and for phrases or clauses. We also use quotation marks for controversial words or for words whose meaning we question (see also Direct and Indirect Speech).

We follow the first set of quotation marks with a capital letter. Furthermore, we follow the second set of quotation marks with a full stop if the quotation *ends* the sentence. In other words, we put the full stop *outside* the quotation marks.
Gemma said: "We need to consider alternative solutions to the problem".

Other punctuation marks

**Apostrophes
(')**

We use the apostrophe in contractions. In other words, we use the apostrophe to indicate that we have *omitted* letters from a word. Contractions are typical of spoken English. Consequently, we can use contractions in our writing to create a conversational tone (see also Verbs and Style and Tone).
We'll *meet on Thursday since* ***you're*** *not available tomorrow.*

We also use apostrophes to indicate *possession*. In other words, we indicate that something belongs to someone or something else by using an apostrophe.
The target of the team becomes *the team**'s** target.*
The brief of the client becomes *the client**'s** brief.*

We use only an apostrophe after plurals which end in -*s* and after plural proper nouns which take a singular verb (see also Nouns and Verbs).
Bosses'; participants'; Reuters'; Barclays'; United States'; and *United Nations'.*

We use apostrophe -*'s* after irregular plurals which do not end in –*s*.
Men's, children's and *media's.*

We use only an apostrophe after a singular word which ends in –*s*.
Boss'; and *Jesus'.*

However, we write *people's* (singular) and *peoples'* (plural).

We use an apostrophe to indicate that we have contracted the verb to the pronoun when we write *it's* (see also Verbs). In other words, *it's*

means *it is*. We use no apostrophe when we use the genitive pronoun *its* to indicate possession (see also Pronouns).
*From now on, **it's** (contraction) going to get harder to compete.*
*We expect the company to increase **its** (pronoun) market share.*

Hyphens
(-)

We use hyphens to form compound adjectives (see also Adjectives).
*A **ten-minute** presentation.*

We also use hyphens to form nouns from phrasal verbs (see also Nouns and Verbs).
*We need **to follow up** (phrasal verb) the survey. **The follow-up** (noun) will be in May.*

Obliques
(/)

We use obliques to mean *or*. Some writers feel that the oblique is awkward. These writers prefer to use the word *or* instead.
*The operator must wear **his/her** gloves when using the machine.*
*The operator must wear **his or her** gloves when using the machine.*

Another alternative which we have is to make the subject of the sentence plural to avoid writing *his or her* (see also Subject and Verb Agreement).
***Operators** must wear **their** gloves when using the machine.*

Ellipsis
(...)

We use ellipsis to indicate that we have omitted some words from a direct quote.
The report said: "The organisation...will cover the cost".

We also use ellipsis to indicate that a sentence or idea is *incomplete*. However, this use of ellipsis has arguably little relevance to business writing. Writers sometimes use ellipsis to attempt to create drama or suspense in creative work or in advertising copy.
You decide if you can afford to ignore this product...

Short cut grammar tips for apostrophes

You can test whether something belongs to someone or something else by changing the *structure* of a sentence.

Change *the teams objectives* to *the objectives of the team*. In this case, *the objectives* clearly belong to *the team*. Consequently, write *team's* with an apostrophe.

Change *the teams attend* to *the attend of the team*. In this case, *attend* is clearly a verb (see also Verbs). Consequently, do not write *teams* with an apostrophe since the word is plural.

Writing tips for punctuation

Use only essential punctuation in business writing. In other words, use punctuation only where punctuation will help your user to make sense of the information on the page.

Write in simple and compound sentences (see also Sentences). Sentences made of only *one or two ideas* are easier for your user to process. Furthermore, shorter sentences require only essential punctuation.

Avoid using contractions in *formal* business writing (see also Verbs). As a result, you will never be confused between *its* and *it's* if you avoid contracting the verb *is* to the pronoun *it* (see also Pronouns).

Joining sentences with a semi-colon or a colon is a sophisticated use of punctuation. You can communicate your message with equal effect by joining your sentences with a conjunction such as *and* (see also Conjunctions). Only join your sentences with a semi-colon or a colon if that style will contribute to your user accepting your message.

Punctuation exercises

Essential exercises

Punctuate the following sentences and short paragraphs. In some cases, you may have more than one alternative. In these cases, the solutions provide a suggested answer only.

1. your appointment is on wednesday 14 april 2001

2. please bring the following to the meeting notebooks pens and diaries

3. we have finished repairing your car and we will deliver the car to you next week

4. the eurolink train leaves from waterloo station at 200pm every day of the week except sunday

5. all consultants will receive a laptop a mobile phone and a fax machine by the end of march next year

6. each country picnic hamper must contain the following items plates napkins glasses and knives and forks

7. the defendant asked lata who had seen the accident to be a witness however lata refused to be involved in the case

8. the national anthropology museum will represent all peoples traditions now since we are aiming for diversity and equality

Bridging exercises Punctuate the following sentences and short paragraphs. In some cases, you may have more than one alternative. In these cases, the solutions provide a suggested answer only.

9. janet white said after coming to the exhibition why did i wait so long to be a part of the project i have so much to gain from being involved

10. the two day conference will take place in berlin in october we hope to organise a follow up conference which will take place some time in the spring

11. the peoples grief and anger has grown steadily at the loss of such an important public figure people expect the government to respond officially before the end of the week

12. the company wants to change location although the risk is considerably higher consequently the senior management team smt needs to meet next week to decide which course of action to take

13. william blackall will give evidence at the trial of jones jones v ungerman a full account of mr blackalls testimony is contained in appendix c mr blackall will appear in court on thursday next week

14. the aircraft left the airport at five o clock that was the last that anyone has seen of the plane since that time the authorities have sent out a search party to see if the teams specialists can find the wreckage

15. representatives from new york moscow paris delhi and london all attended the fourth international conference of alternative representation in rome next year the conference will take place in bombay or sidney

16. all the participants felt that the coaching scheme had helped them in different ways in particular many felt that the scheme had promoted self confidence and self reliance most of the participants were interested in a follow up

Applied exercises Punctuate the following sentences and short paragraphs. In some cases, you may have more than one alternative. In these cases, the solutions provide a suggested answer only.

17. we have decided to move the mens department away from the food department the childrens department will replace the mens department now however the womens department will remain next to the stationery department

18. twenty five million dollars worth of crops has been destroyed by the recent floods which also have destroyed one tenth of all the homes in the area the un has sent troops to help the local community to begin clearing the damage so that people can return home

19. we have performed the following procedures on the property we have inspected the property measured the site made the relevant enquiries and obtained all the necessary information we have listed the current estimate realisation value of the property in table one below

20. the only evidence in support of the charges 6 b 9 c and 12 a is john browns testimony consequently the testimony will be unsupported however john is intelligent and articulate and i expect that he will make an excellent witness nevertheless i encourage the prosecution to find an additional witness as a precaution

21. the development committee has made four decisions everyone must complete a skills inventory form everyone must give their forms to the learning coordinators by friday 4 may the learning coordinators will process all the forms by the end of september this year the committee then will publish the results by the end of the calendar year

22. we have decided to increase the number of high street outlets which we own by 800 units consequently we will need to recruit nearly 3000 new members of staff our urban business expansion report contains a full breakdown of our business proposal including an account of a three stage implementation process our research suggests that the expansion process will take a full year to implement successfully

23. the retail division has seen a steady increase in profits over the last quarter analysts have credited the divisions success to a number of recent acquisitions in particular the division has acquired two new lines of clothing both of which have sold well furthermore the division has launched an in house magazine called fabrication the division designed the magazine to promote the clothing and sales have doubled in the last quarter

24. the urban development proposal recognises that the six areas of the county including middlerow represent a unique social economic and cultural resource the regeneration and redevelopment of these areas will benefit the community in five ways they will meet the development needs of small business people they will maintain investment from larger companies they will enhance the quality of life for local people they will sustain the economy and finally they will relieve development pressures on the countryside

(For answer see pages 209–212)

3.4 **Style and tone**

The function of style and tone

Style and tone are independent but interrelated. In other words, style and tone are two different aspects of writing but style and tone influence each other so much that we have difficulty separating the two. In fact, we could describe style and tone as two sides of the same coin. Consequently, style and tone are *interdependent*.

Style is the *individual words* which a writer chooses to use. Tone is the *emotion* in the words which can be expressed directly or indirectly. However, the tone of a text is determined by the individual words which the writer chooses. As a result, we describe style and tone as interdependent.

Style and tone are hard to assess because different users will respond differently to different words. Consequently, style and tone are often a matter of *interpretation*. What one user may interpret as friendly, another may interpret as disrespectful. Furthermore, in writing we cannot be present to change our approach unlike face-to-face or telephone and video communication. We cannot read the physical signs in the other person and change our style or tone accordingly.

For this reason, business writers need to be clear in their own minds what is their message to others. Writers need to *know* their own message. Moreover, writers need to be equally clear about how they *feel* about their message.

Emotional Intelligence in business writing

Emotional intelligence suggests that people who are effective in communicating with others usually understand the balance between emotion and thought. Successful communicators understand when emotion is appropriate. Just the right amount of emotion can help us to get our message across. Too much or too little emotion can get in the way of communicating effectively. Consequently, good interpersonal skills are as important as acute thinking in business writing to make our message acceptable.

Planning style and tone in our writing

We need to consider three things carefully before writing.

Firstly, who is our *audience*? In other words, who is going to *use* the information? What does our audience *want* to know and what does our audience *need* to know? How can we make our message more real for our audience?

Secondly, what is our *purpose* in sending the message? What *outcome* do we want from the message and how can we measure that outcome?

Finally, what is our *message* and is our message the right message to achieve our purpose? In other words, what is the relationship between our audience, our purpose, and our message?

We are ready to choose the individual words to meet our objectives when we have established these three *guiding principles*. Our objective is always to make our audience accept our message so that we can achieve our purpose.

Ideally, our style should *convey* our message immediately to our user and so achieve our purpose. Our style should never get in the way of the user receiving and accepting our message. Consequently, a style which conveys information clearly and immediately is most appropriate for business writing.

Empowered writers

Empowered writers are capable of being flexible. Empowered writers can adapt their style to suit their user. Empowered writers write for others and not for themselves. Empowered writers make choices about their writing and are unafraid of taking risks. Empowered writers learn from their mistakes and adapt accordingly. Empowered writers recognise that language is alive and that language will be changing always. Empowered writers enjoy the diversity of a wide range writing styles and encourage diversity both in themselves and in other people.

The tools of style and tone

Firstly, we can consider the following stylistic tools to make choices about the tone of our writing.

Plain English

Plain English and shorter words tend to be Anglo-Saxon in origin. Anglo-Saxon words are the words which usually deal with everyday life. Using everyday words will make our writing easier to understand and we are less likely to exclude people. For example, writing *buy* instead of *purchase* will make our writing seem more informal and accessible.

Plain English is most appropriate for texts which need to reach a *wide or undefined audience* or *the general public*. We also can use everyday words effectively in internal documents to *colleagues* and *associates* to create a relaxed or approachable tone. Plain English is also useful for when we write to people from other cultures or languages. In other words, plain English is appropriate for *multicultural* and *multilingual* texts.

However, some audiences expect a level of sophistication. Some words have a wider meaning than their synonyms. Synonyms are different words with the same meaning such as *prison* and *jail*. For example, *commemorating* someone's death is more than merely *remembering* that person.

However, we may choose to develop the complexity of our ideas rather than the complexity of our language if we are writing for a sophisticated or specialised audience. Complex ideas can be expressed still in everyday words.

Nevertheless, we should use our knowledge of our audience always as our *guiding principle*. We are more likely to communicate effectively with someone if we adopt that person's style. For example, using jargon is appropriate for a specialised audience and inappropriate for a public document.

Metaphor   We use metaphor to write about one thing in terms of another thing. In other words, every metaphor has two components. For example, we can write that someone is *as busy as a bee* or *as strong as an ox*.

We call the two components of a metaphor the *vehicle* and the *tenor*. The tenor is the image and the vehicle is how we convey that image. *As busy* (tenor) *as a bee* (vehicle) and *as strong* (tenor) *as an ox* (vehicle).

Typically, we use metaphor in a less obvious way. Usually, we use the tenor alone without the vehicle. We are comparing our profits to a *bird* (vehicle) when we write that our profits are *soaring* (tenor). Furthermore, we are comparing business to *war* (vehicle) when we write that we are *planning our strategy* (tenor).

We use some metaphors so often that we have forgotten that we used these images originally as metaphors. In other words, we take some metaphors for granted. In fact, we have added to the levels of meaning of some words through using those words as metaphors such as *strategy*.

We can use metaphor to make our message more real for our user. Metaphor is particularly appropriate for *marketing copy* and *press releases*. However, we need to consider carefully whether or not our metaphor is appropriate to our user. Furthermore, metaphor is a characteristic of journalism and can create a sensational or dramatic tone in business writing. Consequently, we need to consider carefully whether a sensational or dramatic tone is appropriate for achieving our purpose. We need to ask ourselves again what our user wants and what our user needs to be informed fully.

*Our profits **soared** in the last quarter* (metaphor).

*Our profits **increased by 42%** in the last quarter* (fact).

Metaphor is also useful for motivating and inspiring people in internal communication.

Assertiveness

We say that we are being *assertive* when we display two kinds of behaviour. Firstly, *we recognise our own rights*; and secondly, *we recognise the rights of others*.

Non-assertiveness

We say that we are being *non-assertive* when we display two kinds of behaviour. Firstly, *we deny our own rights*. We call this behaviour *passivity*. Secondly, *we deny the rights of others*. We call this behaviour *aggression*.

Assertiveness in writing

We can be assertive in our business writing if we display the following behaviour. We are assertive if we ask people for what we *need* and if we tell people *why* we need the things which we need. We also should tell people *when* we need the things which we need so that people can decide whether or not they have the time to help us. Furthermore, we need to accept other people's right to say no if those people are unable to help.

We are being assertive also when we recognise our own right to say no to others. However, we should give people *alternatives* when we say no to their requests for help. Giving alternatives helps us to create *win/win* situations.

Characteristics of assertiveness

We respect our own rights. We respect the rights of others. We create win/win situations. We say no if necessary. We provide alternatives when we say no. We thank people for what they have done. We acknowledge achievement. We apologise if we have done wrong. We give explanations if necessary. We provide solutions. We give a point of contact if necessary. We build relationships. We point the way ahead.

Generalisations

Generalisations about any one group of people will offend someone. Only refer to *age, creed, culture, gender, race,* or *sexual orientation* if that reference is *relevant to your message*. Moreover, support any generalisations which are relevant to your message with both evidence and an awareness of prejudice if necessary. However, be aware equally of pressure from interest groups.

Most criminals are young (generalisation).

Eighty-five per cent of offenders are under the age of 25 (fact).

Humour and sarcasm

Humour can help us to relax our users and to warm our users to our message. However, we need to judge our users carefully because we have so many different types of humour. Trying to be funny can work against us if our humour is misjudged or inappropriate. Humour is useful in internal communication as humour can bring people together. Humour is also appropriate in well-established external relationships.

Sarcasm can get in the way of building relationships and we should avoid sarcasm in business writing. We should focus on being *assertive* about anger instead. Irony is subtle and often misunderstood. More importantly, irony is characteristic of British English and is not used or even understood necessarily by other groups of English speakers.

Furthermore, irony is typically difficult for people from other languages and cultures to understand or use. We should assess our users carefully before writing anything which requires reading between the lines. Irony is often culturally relative like humour. What is funny or ironic in one culture can be neither in another culture. Particularly, we need to consider the tools of humour carefully when we are writing for multicultural or multilingual users.

Innuendo and euphemism

We use innuendo to suggest meaning. We should focus on being *assertive* instead. Euphemism is useful for sensitive issues. However, we can use the context of our writing to indicate that we are not necessarily blunt.
*I am sorry to hear that your father **died** last week* (fact).
*I am sorry to hear that your father **passed away** last week* (euphemism).

Hyperbole and understatement

We use hyperbole to *exaggerate* circumstances. In other words, we make circumstances bigger than those circumstances are in reality.
*A **huge amount** (hyperbole) of money is lost **all the time*** (hyperbole).

We use understatement to *reduce* circumstances. In other words, we make circumstances smaller than those circumstances are in reality.
We have a slight (understatement) *problem.*

Hyperbole and understatement are two extremes of each other. We should be specific about quantities because different people attach different meanings to different words. Furthermore, hyperbole and understatement are *culturally* relevant. In other words, different cultures place different values on hyperbole and understatement.

We should try to be *objective* in business writing. We can be objective by focusing on *facts, actions, suggestions, decisions,* and *time-scales.* We can use also *example; analogy; classification; definition;*

explanation; *cause and effect*; *comparison and contrast*; and *process analysis* to support our main point (see also Paragraphs). We can create focus in our writing by omitting any details which do not contribute to our user accepting our message.

An average of a hundred pounds is lost each week (quantified).

We have a problem which will take two weeks to fix (quantified).

Direct and indirect messages

We have two types of messages in writing. The *direct message* is the message which we send in words. The *indirect message* is the overall impression which we give our user.

You will save 10% if you buy now (direct message).

This writer is thoughtful and conscientious (indirect message).

The indirect message which we send to our user may be affected by the *emotional associations* which the user brings to the text. Conversely, we need to be aware of our own emotional associations which we bring to the texts which we produce. An awareness of our own emotional associations will help us to be more objective in both sending and receiving messages.

Positive tone

We can create a positive tone in our writing by avoiding negative statements. Instead, focus on solutions; outcomes; the things which you can achieve, and the things which have gone right. Avoid negative statements and words. Use negative prefixes rather than the word *not* (see also prefixes). A positive tone sends a positive indirect message to your user.

*You can speak to my assistant if I am **not** in* (negative statement) *my office.*

*You can speak to my assistant if I am **out** of* (positive statement) *my office.*

I do not agree (negative statement with *not*).

I disagree (positive statement with prefix).

Emphatic tone

We create an emphatic tone in our writing when we repeat ourselves unnecessarily. We can do a number of things which will create an emphatic tone in our writing. We can use tautology. In other words, we can say the same thing in a different way. We can use a phrasal verb which repeats its meaning. Finally, we can use adverbs such as *actually* and intensifiers such as *really* which make no contribution to meaning. We send an indirect message to our user when we create an emphatic tone in our writing. An emphatic tone implies that we distrust our own ability to communicate effectively.

*We offer a **free complimentary** (tautology) newspaper.*

*We offer a **complimentary** (adjective) newspaper.*

*Use the glue to **join together*** (repetitive phrasal verb) *wood and plastic.*
*Use the glue to **join*** (verb) *wood and plastic.*

*Our clients do not know what we **actually*** (emphatic adverb) *do.*
Our clients do not know what we do (verb).

Grammatical tools

Secondly, we can consider the following grammatical tools to make choices about the style and tone of our writing.

Complete sentences

We can use complete sentences to make our writing *clear* and *action-centred*. A complete sentence must have a subject and a predicate (see also Sentences). A subject is a noun which *performs* the action of the main verb of a sentence (see also Nouns). A predicate is the rest of the sentence including the main verb (see also Verbs). A main verb is a verb which identifies an *action* and a *tense*. The tense indicates *when* an action happened (see also Tense).

Simple, compound, and complex sentences

A simple sentence has at least a subject and a main verb. The sentence can have an object if the main verb is transitive and a predicative adjective if the main verb is intransitive (see also Sentences). *Sarah* (subject) *developed* (main verb – past simple) *the project* (object).

A compound sentence is two or more simple sentences joined with a conjunction such as *and*.
Sarah (subject) *developed* (main verb – past simple) *the project* (object) *and she* (subject) *took* (main verb – past simple) *the project* (object) *to completion.*

A complex sentence can be either a simple or a compound sentence with one or more clauses which contain extra information. Consequently, a complex sentence will have at least a main clause and a subordinate clause.
Sarah developed the project (main clause – simple sentence) *which explored how small business development could be increased in the area* (subordinate defining relative clause).

Embedding

We sometimes *embed* one idea into another. An embedded idea can take the form of a phrase, a clause, or even a simple sentence (see also Phrases and Clauses and Sentences). We create more work for our user when we embed our sentences. Users have to work particularly hard when we separate the subject and the main verb of the sentence with an embedded idea.
The room, and we carefully explored all the options (embedded simple sentence), *was stripped and refitted with wooden panelling* (passive compound sentence).

We explored all the options carefully (simple sentence). *In the end, we decided to strip the room and refit the walls with wooden panelling* (compound sentence).

Contractions We use contractions when we join words by omitting letters. We usually contract the verb to the subject of the sentence. We can omit letters and even syllables from words when we contract words to each other. Consequently, we always show contraction with an apostrophe (see also Punctuation).

I will becomes *I'll*.

You would becomes *you'd*.

He is becomes *he's*.

We are becomes *we're*.

Cannot becomes *can't*.

Phrasal verbs are compound verbs made of a main verb and a preposition such as *stand up* (see also Verbs). We can separate the main verb and the preposition with extra information but main verb and preposition will form a complete phrase still.

*We need to **back** the proposal **up***.

*We need to **back up** the proposal*.

Contractions and phrasal verbs are typical of some forms of spoken English. In written English, contractions and phrasal verbs create a *colloquial* or *conversational* tone (see also Verbs). For this reason, contractions and phrasal verbs are most appropriate to internal documents which are informal such as *memos*. Colleagues from different companies who know each other personally or who have a long working relationship also can use contractions and phrasal verbs effectively.

Some writers feel that the use of some phrasal verbs is poor style. Instead, we can describe phrasal verbs as *emphatic*. In other words, phrasal verbs *emphasise* the action of the main verb. We still can express the action of the main verb clearly without the preposition.

*We need to **back up*** (phrasal verb) *the proposal* (more informal).

*We need to **support*** (verb) *the proposal* (more formal).

Nominalisation We use nominalisation to turn a verb into a noun. We turn verbs into nouns through the technique of word building (see also Nouns and Verbs). We use verbs to identify *actions* and so nominalisation is the process of turning an *action* into a *concept*.

We create a dynamic tone in our writing when we use verbs as verbs. We create a distant tone in our writing when we use verbs as nouns.

The relative pronoun *that*	We make our style more formal when we use the relative pronoun *that* in our sentences (see also Relative Pronouns). Consequently, we make our style more informal or *conversational* when we omit the relative pronoun *that* from our sentences.

*We decided **that** we would change the focus of our investments* (formal).
We decided we would change the focus of our investments (informal).

That and which	We make our style more formal when we use *which* instead of *that* in our sentences (see also Relative Pronouns).

*The package **which** we developed has undergone some changes* (more formal).
*The package **that** we developed has undergone some changes* (less formal).

Who and that	We reify people when we use the relative pronoun *that* instead of the relative pronoun *who* (see also Relative Pronouns). We say that we have reified someone when we turn that person into an object. We say that we have objectified someone when we have made that person objective. In other words, objective is the opposite of subjective.

Alternatively, we personify people when we use the relative pronoun *who*. Personifying people helps to build relationships and creates a personal tone in our writing.
*The man **that** arrived late* (reified) *had to wait until the break.*
*The man **who** arrived late* (personified) *had to wait until the break.*

Ending sentences with a preposition	We make our style conversational when we end our sentences with a preposition (see also Prepositions). Prepositions are words which we use to indicate *position* or *movement*. Alternatively, we make our style formal when we avoid ending a sentence with a preposition.

*The defendant could not remember where he got the information **from*** (conversational).
*The defendant could not remember **from** where he got the information* (formal).

Writing tips for style and tone	Be emotionally intelligent in your business writing. In other words, use an appropriate amount of emotion in your writing to make your message acceptable to your user.

Plan your style and tone before you start writing. Use a style and tone which is appropriate to your objective. Your objective is to make your user accept your message so that you can achieve your purpose.

Use plain English for texts which have a wide or undefined audience. Use plain English for multicultural or multilingual audiences. Use jargon and technical language where appropriate for specialised audiences.

Use metaphor only where metaphor will contribute to you achieving your objectives.

Use an assertive tone in your business writing. In other words, acknowledge your own rights and the rights of others when you are writing.

Avoid generalisations. Use facts if references to *age, creed, culture, gender, race*, or *sexual orientation* are relevant to your message.

Use humour only when humour is appropriate to you achieving your objective. Avoid sarcasm and innuendo. Instead, be assertive. Use irony and euphemism only when irony and euphemism are appropriate to you achieving your objective.

Avoid hyperbole and understatement. Instead, use *facts, actions, suggestions, decisions*, and *time-scales*.

Control your direct message and you will control your indirect message. We send our direct message in words and we *imply* our indirect message as an overall impression.

Create a *positive* tone in your writing by avoiding negative statements and words. Use negative prefixes instead of the word *not* (see also Prefixes).

Avoid an *emphatic* tone in your writing. Avoid tautology, repetitive phrasal verbs, and emphatic adverbs such as *actually*.

Write in complete sentences. Keep your subject and main verb together. Furthermore, put the subject and the main verb in the *first* position in the sentence. Consequently, use the active voice.

Use simple and compound sentences. In other words, limit your sentences to *one or two ideas*.

Avoid embedding phrases, clauses, and even other sentences into your main sentence. Avoid separating your subject and main verb.

Avoid contractions and phrasal verbs in formal business writing. Contractions and phrasal verbs are appropriate to informal or conversational texts.

Use verbs as verbs. In other words, avoid turning verbs into nouns through the process of nominalisation (see also Nouns and Verbs).

Use the relative pronoun *who* instead of the relative pronoun *that* when you refer to people.

Avoid ending sentences with a preposition in formal business writing.

Use only the punctuation which is essential to your user making sense of the information on the page.

Punctuation · We can use essential punctuation only to make our writing clearer and easier to use (see also Punctuation). Simple and compound sentences require little punctuation (see also Sentences).

Style and tone exercises

Essential exercises · Change the style and tone of the following sentences where necessary. The solutions are suggested answers.

---

1. Do you mind writing this proposal for me?

---

2. Write and tell me if you still want the supplies.

---

3. If you have any further queries, please do not hesitate to contact me.

---

4. I know it's a pain but can you return the forms to me as soon as possible.

---

5. Do you think that you could possibly get this work done by some time next week?

---

6. Further to your letter dated 20th August 2002, the Company regrets to inform you that it is unable to process your order.

Bridging exercises · Change the style and tone of the following sentences where necessary. The solutions are suggested answers.

---

7. Stop calling me. You are wasting my time and I have nothing more to say to you on this matter. I have no intention of changing my mind.

---

8. I have a bit of a problem with the printer but I think that I can sort it out. I'll get back to you as soon as I've figured out what to do about the whole thing.

---

9. The garage can't fix your car because we don't have the parts. You'll have to go somewhere else. You have no idea how difficult it is to get the parts you're looking for.

10. The consultants always tell the support staff that they need work done at the last minute and it's not fair. How are we supposed to get all our work done if they just dump things on us?

---

11. A mistake has been made in completing the above order and a replacement has been sent. Should the replacement not be up to standard, return the said replacement to the above address.

---

12. We all know that men cannot express their feelings. You can see this when men are put together in groups to resolve people problems. All the men immediately start focussing purely on the processes of management.

Applied exercises

Change the style and tone of the following sentences where necessary. The solutions are suggested answers.

13. I cannot tell you how terribly sorry I am that I did not e-mail you back straight away but you know how things get at this time of year. I just haven't had even a moment to myself. So once again, I'm sorry about the delay.

---

14. It is incumbent on all members of staff to take telephone enquiries. Furthermore, it is the responsibility of all members of staff to inform others of their whereabouts should they not be present at their workstation to answer the telephone.

---

15. I want the report immediately. You will have to drop everything else that you are doing to get it finished. You will have to reassess your priorities if you cannot get it finished on time. Furthermore, I expect the work to be perfect since this is a very important client.

---

16. I know that your father died recently but the project is starting next week and I have to know whether or not you're going to get on board. A number of other people have expressed interest so I doubt that you can afford to miss this opportunity. Let me know by tomorrow.

17. I will not tolerate people arriving late for the presentations. Do people not realise how difficult it is to speak when other people are walking into the room all the time? If you have no respect for the work of others, then have the decency not to attend rather than interrupting the speaker or the presentation.

18. Every month we have exactly the same situation with the expenses. Consultants are always late with their claims and we always have to run after people to find out how much they are claiming so that we can work out our departmental costs. We are not going to put up with this any more. From now on, any consultant who doesn't claim expenses by the 25th will pay a 5% fee.

(For answers see pages 213–215)

3.5 **Review**

Sentences and paragraphs

We looked in Section Three at how we form sentences into units of information called paragraphs. We established that shorter paragraphs are more inviting to the user. We saw also that we should block and space our paragraphs to make them easier to use. Furthermore, we should left-justify our paragraphs so that our paragraphs are easier to proofread.

Characteristics of paragraphs

We established that each new topic or each new angle on a topic should have its own paragraph. We also established that each paragraph should have a topic sentence. The topic sentence provides an overview for the user of what the paragraph contains. The topic sentence is usually the first sentence of a paragraph.

Cohesion and coherence in paragraphs

Furthermore, we looked at ways in which we can bind information both within paragraphs and between paragraphs. We call this textual quality cohesion and coherence. Cohesion is how the ideas in a text fit and coherence is how the writer makes sense of the information for the user. We established that we can use keywords, linking words, paragraphs, metaphors, images, subheadings, summaries, introductions, conclusions, and main headings to bind a text.

Punctuation

We moved from paragraphs to punctuation. Firstly, we established that we use punctuation to help our user make sense of the information on the page. Then we looked in detail at all the punctuation marks which we use in English. We should use punctuation only when the punctuation contributes to how the user makes sense of the information. We also saw that we can keep our punctuation to the minimum if we write in a clear and brief style.

Style and tone

Finally, we looked at the relationship between style and tone. We explored how style and tone are *interdependent* since style and tone create each other. We saw that an assertive tone which understands the user's needs and wants is best suited to business writing. More importantly, we saw that we should use style and tone to meet our objective in writing. In other words, our style and tone should be *appropriate* to making our user accept our message so that we can achieve our purpose.

The final self-assessment Now all that remains is for you to do is to complete the Final Self-Assessment of The Workbook. The Final Self-Assessment covers all the essentials of grammar with which you should be confident in order to be in control of your writing.

Appendices

A Final self-assessment

Arrange the following words into the labelled boxes below.

half	its	your	across	selling
behind	never	sunk	so	furthermore
managed	but	frankly	that	massive
who	quarter	under	well	whose
firstly	finally	one-fifth	four	one-and-a-half
in	to	marketable	they	above
often	you're	from	after	always
second	on	blow-up	thirdly	shares
and	three-quarters	if	alternatively	five
leader	while	during	over	myself
or	first	however	walk out	because
it's	me	their	useful	consequently
between	annually	before	frequently	next to
nevertheless	in front	rarely	been	ever
six	also	margins	moreover	lastly
which	speak	through	two-thirds	profit
below	yourselves	done	mine	us
seldom	index	third	quarterly	have
his	last	whom	management	stylish

Nouns

[ ]

Pronouns

[ ]

Adjectives

```



```

Prepositions

```



```

Verbs

```



```

Adverbs

```



```

Numerals

```



```

Conjunctions

```



```

Change the following into complete sentences where necessary.

The delivery and presentation of material on the fourth floor of Office Block Nine at four o'clock on Thursday afternoon.

The buying and selling of stock by the production team for the last eight months in different business districts in the City.

Change the following so that the subject and the verb agree where necessary.

What does eight plus four equal?

_____

"People" are the subject of the sentence.

_____

There are a number of choices open to us.

_____

The media is responsible for not printing unauthorised photographs.

Change the following into the active voice where necessary.

The boxes are stacked by the doorway.

_____

It is thought that the best approach is to raise costs.

_____

The rising and falling of profits over the last quarter mean that predictions are unreliable.

Punctuate the following sentences where necessary.

---

the senior management team smt needs to consider carefully the following issues the majority of staff prefers flexible working hours many people want more freedom to make decisions in their daily work and a day care centre would benefit those with young children the smt will address each of these issues in detail at next weeks meeting however the team has made no commitments yet to any outcomes

B Final self-assessment solution

Arrange the following words into the labelled boxes below.

half	its	your	across	selling
behind	never	sunk	so	furthermore
managed	but	frankly	that	massive
who	quarter	under	well	whose
firstly	finally	one-fifth	four	one-and-a-half
in	to	marketable	they	above
often	you're	from	after	always
second	on	blow-up	thirdly	shares
and	three-quarters	if	alternatively	five
leader	while	during	over	myself
or	first	however	walk out	because
it's	me	their	useful	consequently
between	annually	before	frequently	next to
nevertheless	in front	rarely	been	ever
six	also	margins	moreover	lastly
which	speak	through	two-thirds	profit
below	yourselves	done	mine	us
seldom	index	third	quarterly	have
his	last	whom	management	stylish

Nouns

half	quarter	blow-up	mine	shares
second	while	margins	management	profit
leader	index	well	selling	

Pronouns

who	its	your	that	whose
which	me	their	they	myself
his	yourselves	whom	mine	us

Adjectives

managed	first	marketable	well	massive
second	last	third	useful	stylish
			quarterly	

Prepositions

behind	below	in front	during	over
in	to	under	through	above
between	on	from	across	next to

Verbs

managed	you're	sunk	been	shares
second	speak	done	mine	profit
it's	index	walk out	selling	have
	last			

Adverbs

firstly	never	frankly	well	quarterly
often	finally	during	after	always
seldom	while	before	thirdly	ever
	annually	rarely	frequently	lastly

Numerals

second	three-quarters	one-fifth	four	one-and-a-half
six	first	third	two-thirds	five

Conjunctions

firstly	but	however	alternatively	because
and	finally	so	moreover	consequently
or	also	thirdly	furthermore	lastly
nevertheless	if			

Change the following into complete sentences where necessary.

The delivery and presentation of material on the fourth floor of Office Block Nine at four o'clock on Thursday afternoon.

The sales consultant (subject) will deliver and present (main verb – future simple) the material on the fourth floor of Office Block Nine. The presentation (subject) will take place (main verb – future simple) at four o'clock on Thursday afternoon.

The buying and selling of stock by the production team for the last eight months in different business districts in the city.

The production team (subject) has bought and sold (main verb – present perfect) stock for the last eight months. The team (subject) has been working (main verb – present perfect continuous) in different business districts in the City.

Change the following so that the subject and the verb agree where necessary.

What *do* (plural main verb – present simple) *eight plus four* (plural subject) equal?

"People" (singular subject) *is* (singular main verb – present simple) the subject of the sentence.

The *subject* (singular subject) of the sentence *is* (singular main verb – present simple) "people".

There (empty subject) *is* (singular main verb – present simple) a number of choices open to us.

A *number* (singular subject) of choices *is* (singular main verb – present tense) open to us.

We (plural subject) *have* (plural main verb – present tense) a number of choices open to us.

The *media* (collective noun – singular subject) *is* (singular main verb – present simple) responsible for not printing unauthorised photographs.

Change the following into the active voice where necessary.

The *boxes* (subject) *are* (intransitive main verb – present simple) *stacked by the doorway* (predicative adjective).

It (empty object) *is thought* (passive main verb – present simple) that the best approach is to raise costs.

The *Board members* (subject) *think* (active main verb – present simple) that the best approach is to raise costs.

The *rising and falling* (subject) of profits over the last quarter mean (active main verb – present simple) that *predictions* (subject) *are* (active main verb – present simple) *unreliable* (predicative adjective).

Punctuate the following sentences where necessary.

(T)he (S)enior (M)anagement (T)eam (SMT) needs to consider carefully the following issues(:) the majority of staff prefers flexible working hours(;) many people want more freedom to make decisions in their daily work(;) and a day(-)care centre would benefit those with young children(.) (T)he (S)(M)(T) will address each of these issues in detail at next week(')s meeting(.) (H)owever(,) the (T)eam has made no commitments yet to any outcomes(.)

C Conclusion to The Workbook

The need to be in control of our writing

We established at the start of The Workbook that we need to be in control of our writing in today's business world. We are all under pressure and controlled writing saves time and effort. Furthermore, we tend to *use* business documents rather than *read* business documents because of our time and workload pressure. Consequently, clear and immediate messages are easier for us to use.

The relationship between thinking and writing

We established that a *relationship* exists between thinking and writing. Furthermore, we established that clear writing is the result of clear thinking. We need to be clear about our objectives before we start writing if we want our writing to be effective. We can think of our objectives as our *guiding principles*. We have three guiding principles. Firstly, who is going to use our information? Secondly, what is our purpose in writing? Finally, what is our message to our user and how does our content support our message?

The route of acquisition

We continued by establishing that we can use our knowledge of grammar to control our writing. The structure of grammar reflects the way in which we make sense of the world. Consequently, I have followed more or less *the route of acquisition* in The Workbook. The route of acquisition is the path by which we learn our first and subsequent languages. The route represents also the way in which we make sense of information for other people.

The structure of The Workbook

Consequently, we have examined the types of words which we use; how we form those words into different types of sentences; and how we form those types of sentences into paragraphs. We looked also at punctuation and style and tone as part of the process of structuring information into paragraphs.

The relevance of grammar to business writing

I have tried to relate the grammar points to business writing throughout The Workbook. Furthermore, I have tried to translate each grammar point into a style tip for business writers. We have examined style from the point of view of using a style which is *appropriate* to achieving the purpose of our document. Consequently, I have focused on the *effect* which particular grammar structures will have on our style. We create our style through our use of grammar and vocabulary. Consequently, I have tried to demonstrate in The Workbook that an awareness of grammar will put you in control of your writing. Finally, remember that a writer who is in control of his or her writing is a writer in control of his or her message.

D Glossary of grammatical and linguistic terms

The scope of the glossary The following glossary is limited to only the grammar and language terms which I have used in The Workbook. Consequently, the glossary refers almost exclusively to written language.

The type of definitions in the glossary I have tried where possible to avoid using grammar terms to explain other grammar terms. However, detailed explanations are often impossible because of space. I have provided no examples in this glossary for the same reason. You will have to find the terms in The Workbook to clarify their meaning further.

How to use the glossary The glossary provides the terms in alphabetical groups for easy access. Scan the glossary to find the terms about which you would like to find more information. Then look in the Table of Contents at the front of The Workbook to find the term and the corresponding page number. You will be able then to study the term in more detail in the appropriate section.

Abbreviation The *shortening* of a word sometimes as a series of upper case letters which we call an acronym.

Abstract noun A word which identifies an *emotion, value, principle, quality,* or *concept* which we can *experience* but not touch.

Active voice A sentence where we see the subject *actively* performing the main verb.

Adjective A word which *describes* an object.

Adjectival phrase A *group* of words which tells us more information about a noun. We also call these phrases *predicative adjectives*.

Adverb of manner A word which describes *how* someone or something performs an action.

Adverb of place A word which describes *where* someone or something performs an action.

Adverb of time A word which describes *when* someone or something performs an action.

Adverb A word which *describes* an action.

Adverbial A phrase or group of words which *describes* an action.

Apostrophe A punctuation mark which indicates *possession* and where we have omitted letters from words in contractions.

Auxiliary verb	A small verb which helps the main verb of a sentence in verbs of more than one word or compound verbs.
Cardinal number	Numbers which tell us about *quantity* and which start from and include zero.
Causative verb	A word which describes an action which we cause *someone* else to perform for us.
Clause	A *group* of words which usually includes a main verb and possibly a subject but which is part of a larger sentence.
Closed class of word	A class of word to which we can add no new words.
Closed question	A question form which we use to clarify *specific* information and which has a *yes* or *no* answer.
Coherence	A quality which makes a text *understandable*.
Cohesion	A quality which *binds* a text.
Collective noun	A word which names a *group* of people, animals, or objects.
Colloquial style	The choice of words which will make writing seem like a *conversation*.
Comma	A punctuation mark which we use to indicate that we have added *extra information* to a sentence.
Common noun	A word which identifies an *everyday* object.
Comparative adjective	A word which *compares* the qualities of one object to the qualities of another object.
Comparative adverb	A word which *compares* the nature of one action to the nature of another action.
Complex sentence	A sentence with *one or more* clauses which provide extra information to the main point of the sentence.
Compound adjective	A word which describes an object and which is made of *more than one* word joined by a hyphen.
Compound object	More than one person, animal, or thing which *receive* the action of the main verb of a sentence.
Compound sentence	Two or more simple sentences joined with a conjunction such as *and*.
Compound subject	More than one person, animal, or thing which *perform* the action of the main verb of a sentence.
Concrete noun	A word which identifies things which we can *touch*.
Conjugation	The process by which we change the main verb to match the subject of the sentence.
Conjunction	A word which we use to *join* sentences.
Conjunctive adverb	A word which we use to join sentences and which describes the *time*, *place*, or *manner* of that joining.
Conjunctive phrase	A *group* of words without a main verb which we use to join sentences or paragraphs.

Consonants	The twenty-one letters of the English alphabet which are other than the five vowels a, e, i, o, and u.
Contraction	The *shortening* of the auxiliary or modal verb to the subject which is typical of spoken English and *informal* writing.
Conversational style	The choice of words which will make writing seem like a *conversation*.
Copular verb	A word which identifies a *state* such as to *be* and which introduces a *description* of the *subject* of the sentence.
Countable noun	A word which identifies an object of which we can have *more than one*.
Dash	A punctuation mark which we use to indicate that we have added *extra information* to a sentence.
Defining relative clause	A group of words which adds information which *identifies* the subject of a sentence.
Definite article	We have only *one* definite article which is **the**.
Demonstrative adjective	We have only *four* demonstrative adjectives which are **this**, **that**, **these**, and **those**.
Determiner	We have only *four* determiners which are **this**, **that**, **these**, and **those**.
Direct speech	The written form of the *exact* words which someone has spoken.
Ellipses	Punctuation marks which we use to indicate that we have *omitted* information from a sentence.
Embedding	A style where we insert phrases, clauses, and sentences of extra information between the subject and main verb.
Emphatic tone	The emotion which we create in our writing when we repeat ourselves unnecessarily.
Exclamation mark	The punctuation mark which we use to indicate the end of an *exclamatory* statement.
Finite verb	A word which identifies an action and which also tells us *when* that action happens.
Formal style	The choice of words which makes writing seem *formal*.
Fractional number	A number *less* than one and *more* than zero.
Full stop	A punctuation mark which we use to indicate that a sentence has come to an *end*.
Genitive pronoun	A word which indicates *possession* and which we use to replace a noun.
Gerund	A word which looks like a continuous tense verb with an *–ing* ending but which *functions* as a noun.
Hyphen	A punctuation mark which we use to join different words into a *single* form.

Imperative mood	A sentence structure which has the tone of a command.
Indefinite article	We have only *two* indefinite articles which are **a** and **an**.
Indirect speech	The written form of the words which someone has said and which we tell someone else and often paraphrase.
Infinitive verb	A word which identifies an action but *without* telling us when that action happens.
Informal style	The choice of words which makes writing seem *informal*.
Interrogative pronoun	A word which we use to ask an open *question* for general information.
Intransitive verb	A word which identifies a *state of being* and so we cannot transfer the action to an object in the sentence.
Jargon	A word which we use inside a *specialised* field of knowledge.
Keywords	Words which are central to a user's understanding of a text.
Linking words	A word or group of words which we use to join sentences or paragraphs.
Metaphor	A poetic device which we use to compare a quality of one object to the quality of another.
Modal verb	A word which changes the main verb of a sentence to indicate *possibility*, *permission*, *certainty*, *obligation*, or *intention*.
Mood	The tone of a sentence created through a specific use of grammar.
Negative statement	A statement in a negative form.
Nominalisation	The *process* of changing a verb into a noun by adding a suffix to the end of the verb.
Non-defining relative clause	A group of words which adds information which does *not* identify the subject of a sentence.
Noun	A word which *identifies* an object.
Noun phrase	A *group* of words which identifies and describes a noun.
Object	A word which indicates the person, animal, or thing which *receives* the action of the main verb of a sentence.
Object pronoun	A word which we use to *replace* the noun when the noun is the object of a sentence.
Oblique	A punctuation mark which we use to mean *or*.
Open class of word	A class of word to which we can add *new* words.
Open question	A question form which we use to ask for *unspecified or general* information.

Ordinal number	A word which tell us the *order* or *sequence* of a series of numbers.
Paragraph	A *group* of sentences bound by a common topic.
Parentheses	Punctuation marks which we use to indicate that we have added *extra information* to a sentence.
Particle	A syllable which we put *in front* or *behind* a root word to change the word's class or tense.
Passive participle	A syllable which we put *behind* a main verb to change the verb into the passive voice.
Passive verb	A main verb which we attach to the object of the sentence but which the subject still performs.
Passive voice	A sentence where the subject *passively* performs the main verb.
Past participle	A syllable which we put *behind* a main verb to change the verb into the past tense.
Personal pronoun	A word which we use to replace a noun which refers to someone or something.
Phrasal verb	A group of words made of a main verb with a tense and *one or more* prepositions.
Phrase	A group of words *without* a main verb which is a verb with a tense.
Possessive adjective	A word which describes a noun by indicating that the noun *belongs* to someone or something.
Possessive pronoun	A word which we use to replace a noun and which indicates that the noun *belongs* to someone or something.
Predicate	*All* the information in a sentence other the subject.
Predicative adjective	A *group* of words which describes a noun and which follows a main verb which describes a state of being.
Prefix	A syllable which we put *in front* of a root word to change the word's meaning or function.
Preposition	A word which indicates the *position* or *movement* of someone or something.
Prepositional phrase	A group of words which a preposition introduces.
Present participle	The *–ing* suffix which we add to the end of a main verb to form the continuous tense.
Proper noun	A word which refers to the *official name* of a person, animal, or thing.
Punctuation	The marks which we use to organise words into sentences so that we can make *sense* of information.
Question mark	The punctuation mark which we use to indicate the *end* of a question.
Reflexive pronoun	A word which we use to indicate that the subject of a sentence both performs an action and receives that same action.

Relative clause	A group of words which we *add* to a sentence to tell us extra information about the main idea of the sentence.
Root word	A word to which we add a prefix at the start or a suffix at the end to change the word's *meaning* or *function*.
Semantics	The study of meaning.
Semi-formal style	The choice of words which makes writing seem *semi-formal*.
Signposting	A *technique* by which we indicate to a user how the information in our text fits.
Simple sentence	A group of words with a subject, a main verb, and possibly an object or a predicative adjective.
Singular expression	An expression such as *everyone* which we can use to refer to a group but which is always singular.
Speech verb	A word which identifies *how* someone spoke a particular sentence and which we use with direct and indirect speech.
Split infinitive	An adverb which we put *between* the preposition *to* and the verb of an infinitive verb.
Standard English	A form of English which contains *no variations* of any particular dialect, slang, or speech pattern.
Style	The individual words which writers *choose* and how writers arrange those words in sentences.
Subject	The person, animal, or thing which performs the *action* of the main verb of a sentence.
Subject and verb agreement	The noun which performs the action of a sentence should agree with the main verb in *person* and *number*.
Subject pronoun	A word which we use to *replace* the noun when the noun performs the main verb of a sentence.
Subordinate clause	A group of words which provides extra information which supports the main point of a sentence.
Suffix	A syllable which we put *behind* a root word to change the word's *meaning* or *function*.
Superlative adjective	A word which *compares* the quality of someone or something to the qualities of three or more other people or things.
Superlative adverb	A word which *compares* the nature of an action to the nature of three or more other actions.
Syllable	A group of letters which creates the units which are the components of words.
Synonym	A word which has the *same* or *similar* meaning to a different word.
Tautology	Unnecessary repetition.
Tenor	The quality of an object which we compare to another object when we create a metaphor.
Text	A body of writing.

Tone	The *emotion* in a sentence or a text.
Topic	The subject of discussion in a paragraph or text.
Topic sentence	A sentence which *establishes* what a paragraph or text discusses.
Transitive verb	A word which identifies an action which we can *transfer* to someone or something else.
Uncountable noun	A word which identifies something which we cannot *quantify* or of which we cannot have more than one.
Vehicle	The image which we use to carry a comparison in a metaphor.
Verb	A word which identifies an *action* or a *state of being*.
Verb phrase	A group of words which tells us more about an action.
Vocabulary	The words which we use in a language.
Vowel	The *five* letters *a, e, i, o,* and *u.*
Word combinations	Words which we typically combine and which consist usually of an open class word and a preposition.
Word	A group of letters which form a unit and which has a meaning which we agree by *convention.*
Word building	The *process* by which we create new words by adding prefixes and suffixes to root words.

E Writing tips summary

1 The parts of speech

Short cut grammar tips for nouns	We can test a noun by putting an article such as *a, an, or the* in front of the word. *A book*; *an envelope*; or *the pen* (see also Articles). Sometimes we use the same word both as a verb and as a noun (see also Verbs). Consequently, we need to focus on how words *function* in sentences rather than on what words *mean*. *I am going on **a walk*** (noun). *I am going **to walk*** (verb). We can identify a gerund by looking to see whether or not the auxiliary verb *to be* precedes the word (see also Verbs). ***The*** (article) ***lowering*** (gerund) *of costs is the priority of the team.* *The department manager **is** (auxiliary verb to be) **lowering** (continuous tense verb) the cost of production.*
Writing tips for nouns	Using nominalisation will create a more formal style to your writing and so a more formal tone. In other word, your writing will be more *distant* if you use verbs as nouns (see Nominalisation). ***The meeting*** (gerund) *of clients is restricted to the rooms on the third floor.* Using verbs as verbs will create a more action-centred style in your writing and so a more action-centred tone. In other words, your writing will be more *dynamic* if you use verbs as verbs (see also Verbs). *We expect consultants **to meet** (verb) their clients only in the rooms on the third floor.*

Writing tips for pronouns

Avoid confusing the subject pronoun *I* with the object pronoun *me* in compound subjects and compound objects (see also Sentences).

We write *Harold and I went to the meeting* because we write *I went to the meeting*.

Moreover, we write *Pamela met Harold and me in the reception* because we write *Pamela met me in the reception* (see also Subject and Verb Agreement).

Avoid using the reflexive pronoun in the place of the object pronoun (see also Reflexive Pronouns).

Write *I have sent this to yourselves* as *I have sent this to you*.

Avoid using the reflexive pronoun for *emphasis*. An emphatic tone implies that the user understands the context of the situation. Instead, *articulate* clearly the point of your statement.

The consultant had to do the work herself (emphatic tone).

The consultant had to do the work and so we wasted time which we could have used more productively (articulate tone).

Writing tips for relative pronouns

Use the relative pronoun *who* for people. We reify people when we use the relative pronoun *that* for a person. We say that we have reified someone when we have turned that person into an object.

We asked the man that arrived late to wait (reified).

We asked the man who arrived late to wait (personified).

Use the relative pronoun *which* to make your writing *more* formal. Use the relative pronoun *that* to make your writing *less* formal.

We will reward the team which comes first (more formal).

We will reward the team that comes first (less formal).

Use the object relative pronoun *whom* to make your writing *more formal*. Furthermore, you can avoid ending a sentence with a preposition if you use the object relative pronoun *whom* (see also Prepositions). Use the subject relative pronoun *who* for the object of the sentence to make your writing *more conversational*.

Can you tell me to whom I should send the package? (Formal)

Can you tell me who I should send the package to? (Conversational)

Short cut grammar tips for adjectives

Test a word to see if the word is an adjective by putting the word in the position of the predicate of the sentence (see also Sentences).

The blue form becomes *the form is blue*.

The hardworking team becomes *the team is hardworking*.

Writing tips for adjectives

Consider carefully the number of adjectives which you use in business writing. Sometimes we can obscure the subject of the sentence with too many adjectives. Remember the guideline of limiting your sentences to one or two *ideas* (see also Sentences).

Use only the adjectives which give the user *essential information* about the subject. Ask yourself what the user needs to know so that he or she can *understand* and *accept* your message.

Writing tips for articles and determiners

We use the object pronoun *them* instead of the determiner *those* in some forms of spoken English. We say *hand me **them** books*. A plural determiner would be more appropriate since we use Standard English in business writing. Write instead *hand me **those** books*.

Writing tips for prepositions

Some people think that finishing a sentence with a preposition is incorrect. However, perhaps we could describe this style more accurately as being typical of spoken English. Avoid finishing your sentences with a preposition if you choose to use a formal style in your writing.
What did you put the papers in? (Informal style)
In what did you put the papers? (Formal style)

Write as you speak if you choose to use an informal or conversational style in your writing. In other words, finishing your sentences with a preposition would create a relaxed and informal style. Establish your purpose clearly before you start writing and then allow your style to follow from the guiding principle of your purpose.
To whom did you speak? (Formal style)
Who did you speak to? (Informal or conversational style)
(See also Relative Pronouns for the last example)

Some people consider the use of phrasal verbs to be a symptom of a lazy writing style. However, perhaps we could describe phrasal verbs better as *emphatic*. In other words, we use phrasal verbs for *emphasis*. Phrasal verbs tend to be characteristic of spoken English and so we can use phrasal verbs to create an informal style in our writing.

Consider carefully the context of your writing. Use a main verb alone if the *meaning* of the action is clear. In other words, use a phrasal verb only if the preposition will *clarify* the meaning of the main verb. For example, *report* and *report back* mean the same thing as do *join* and *join together*. However, *stand* could mean *stand up* or *stand out* and *sit* could mean *sit down* or *sit up* (see also Style and Tone).

Short cut grammar tips for verbs	We can test a word to see if the word is a verb by putting the preposition *to* in front of the word. In other words, we can turn a verb into the verb's *infinitive* form. We can write *to walk* and *to type* but not *to car* or *to cat*.

Writing tips for verbs	Avoid splitting the infinitive verb with an adverb in formal business writing such as *to quickly write*. Instead, put the adverb *before* or *after* the infinitive verb such as *quickly to write* or *to write quickly*. However, remember also that currently grammarians consider the split infinitive to be a mark of poor style rather than a mark of poor grammar.
	Put an adverb *before* or *after* the compound verb such as **desperately** *has been trying* or *has been trying* **desperately** to create a more formal tone in your writing. Putting an adverb inside a compound verb such as *has* **desperately** *been trying* or *has been trying* **desperately** will create a conversational tone in your writing. However, we always form negative compound verbs by putting the negative word *not* inside the compound verb. We *write has **not** been trying*.
	Avoid misplacing the adverb in a sentence by attaching the adverb to the wrong verb (see also Adverbs). *John **only** cares for numbers* means that John does nothing else with numbers except care for them. *John cares for numbers **only*** means that John cares for nothing else except numbers.
	Avoid contracting the verb to the subject of a sentence in formal business writing such as *I'll* and *you're*. However, contractions can be useful for informal business writing because contractions create a conversational tone.

Short cut grammar tips for adverbs	We can test a word to see if the word is an adverb by asking whether the word tells us *when*, *where*, or *how* we perform an action.
	Adverbs of manner indicate how we perform actions and usually end in the suffix –*ly*. *Slowly*, *quickly* and ***courageously***.

Writing tips for adverbs

Avoid splitting the infinitive verb with an adverb in formal business writing such as *to quickly write*. Instead, put the adverb *before* or *after* the infinitive verb such as *quickly to write* or *to write quickly*. However, remember also that currently grammarians consider the split infinitive to be a mark of poor style rather than a mark of poor grammar.

Put an adverb *before* or *after* the compound verb such as ***desperately** has been trying* or *has been trying **desperately*** to create a more formal tone in your writing. Putting an adverb inside a compound verb such as *has **desperately** been trying* or *has been trying **desperately*** will create a more conversational tone in your writing. However, we always form negative compound verbs by putting the negative word *not* inside the compound verb. We *write has **not** been trying*.

Avoid misplacing the adverb of a sentence by attaching the adverb to the wrong verb (see also Adverbs). *John **only** cares for numbers* means that John does nothing else with numbers except care for them. *John cares for numbers **only*** means that John cares for nothing else except numbers.

Good is an adjective but not an adverb. However, *well* is an adverb and also an adjective. Finally, *deadly* is an adjective and *fatally* is an adverb.

Writing tips for numerals

Write cardinal numbers *between zero and ten* as words.

Write cardinal numbers *from 11 onwards* as figures.

Always write a number as a word if the number *starts* a sentence.

Always *hyphenate* compound numerals or numbers made of *more than one* numeral.

Use no abbreviations for dates which *include* the month.

Use abbreviations for dates which *do not include* the month to indicate to your user that the figure is a date and not a quantity.

Writing tips for conjunctions

Some people think that we should not use a conjunction to start a sentence. However, we should consider starting a sentence with a conjunction as an issue of *style* rather than of *grammar*.

Consider the *effect* which starting a sentence with a conjunction will have on the tone of a piece of writing. Sentences which start with conjunctions seem more conversational. These sentences imitate spoken English and so are more informal.

Avoid starting a sentence with a conjunction in *formal* business writing, since the function of a conjunction is to join. Consider using a conjunctive adverb instead.
But (conjunction) *we should consider still the impact of the decision.*
However (conjunctive adverb), *we should consider still the impact of the decision.*

The exception to the guideline of not starting a sentence with a conjunction is the conjunction *if*. We use the conjunction *if* to join the conditional clause of a conditional sentence to the action clause (see also Modals and Conditionals).
If you have any questions (conditional clause), *please contact me on 0171 444 5555* (action clause).

Consequently, we can start a sentence acceptably with the conjunction *if* when the sentence is conditional. However, the sentence will be more direct if we put the action clause first and then the conditional clause. We can avoid starting a sentence with a conjunction also in this form.
Please contact me on 0171 444 5555 (action clause) *if you have any questions* (conditional clause).

Writing tips for conjunctive adverbs

We begin the conjunctive adverb with a capital letter and we follow the conjunctive adverb with a comma when we start a sentence with a conjunctive adverb.

We need the stock immediately. **However,** *we only have storage space for half of the stock which we need.*

We end the first sentence with semi-colon; we start the conjunctive adverb with a small letter; and we follow the conjunctive adverb with a comma when we join two sentences with a conjunctive adverb.

We need the stock immediately; **however,** *we only have storage space for half of the stock which we need.*

We use conjunctive adverbs to *start* sentences and to *join* sentences. However, we should try to avoid using conjunctive adverbs in the *middle* of sentences in formal business writing. Nevertheless, the position of a conjunctive adverb is an issue of *style* rather than of *grammar*. Putting a conjunctive adverb in the *middle* of a sentence is typical of spoken English. We can consider a conversational style as *inappropriate* to formal business writing (see also Style and Tone).

We can argue that we should avoid putting a conjunctive adverb in the *middle* of a sentence since we would never put a conjunction in a similar position.

We need the stock immediately. We only have storage space, **however** (conjunctive adverb), *for half of the stock which we need.*
We need the stock immediately. We only have storage space **but** (conjunction) *for half of the stock which we need.*

Writing tips for conjunctive phrases

Use conjunctive phrases to start sentences and always end a conjunctive phrase with a comma (see also Phrases and Clauses and Punctuation).
On the other hand, we should consider carefully how our competitors will respond.

Avoid separating subjects and main verbs with a conjunctive phrase (see also Nouns and Verbs and Sentences). Instead, put the conjunctive phrase in the *first* position of the sentence and keep the subject and main verb together.
*The team (subject), **as a result**, needs (main verb) to work harder.*
***As a result**, the team (subject) needs (main verb) to work harder.*

Avoid separating compound verbs with a conjunctive phrase (see also Verbs). Instead, put the conjunctive phrase in the *first* position of the sentence and keep the compound verb together.
*The department **has**, in other words, **been developing** (compound verb) a new system.*
*In other words, the department **has been developing** (compound verb) a new system.*

2 Groups of words

Writing tips for phrases and clauses

Be aware of creating complex subjects when you use phrases to provide extra information about the subject of a sentence. A complex subject is a subject made of a phrase or a clause rather than a word. Using complex subjects can lead easily to mistakes with subject and verb agreement.

Always use a comma after a conjunctive phrase (see also Punctuation).

Avoid using non-defining relative clauses because these clauses separate the subject and the main verb of a sentence. Instead, use the non-defining relative clause as a separate sentence.

Put the main clause of a complex sentence first and then follow with the subordinate clause. The sentence will be more direct with the main clause in the first position.

Put the action clause before the condition clause in a conditional sentence. The sentence will be more direct with the action clause in the first position. Moreover, you also will avoid starting the sentence with the conjunction *if*.

Short cut grammar tip for direct and indirect objects

Rewrite the sentence in the passive voice if you have difficulty in identifying the direct and indirect object of a sentence. The order of a passive sentence is object, main verb, and subject (see also Active and Passive Voice).

I (subject) *gave* (transitive main verb) *him* (indirect object) *the ultimatum* (direct object).
The ultimatum (direct object) *was given* (passive main verb) *to him* (indirect object) *by me* (subject).

Writing tips for sentences

Limit your sentences to *one or two ideas* since long sentences are difficult to understand. In other words, write in simple and compound sentences. Another guideline would be to limit your sentences to *between twelve and eighteen words* since shorter sentences are easier to process.

Put the subject and verb in the *first position* in the sentence whenever possible. Keep the subject and the verb together and put extra information at the end of the sentence. In other words, avoid embedding extra information between the subject and the main verb. Put the *main idea* first as the main clause and then put the *supporting idea* in the second position as the subordinate clause (see also Phrases and Clauses).

Use the imperative mood for *instructions* and *procedures*. Use the word *please* to create a more personal tone if necessary (see also Style and Tone).

Short cut grammar tip for tense

Verbs which follow the third person singular pronouns *he/she/it* always end in the suffix *−s* in the present tense only.
He writes; she directs; and it cleans.

Writing tips for tense

Avoid separating compound verbs with adverbs in formal business writing.
*Catherine **has been** desperately **trying** to finish the project.*
*Catherine **has** desperately **been trying** to finish the project.*

Instead, put the adverb before or after the compound verb.
*Catherine **has been trying** desperately to finish the project.*
*Catherine **has been trying** to finish the project desperately.*
(See also Compound Verbs and Adverbs).

Writing tips for subject and verb agreement

Keep the subject and the main verb of the sentence together to make fewer subject and verb agreement mistakes. Furthermore, write in the active voice to make fewer subject and verb agreement mistakes (see also Active and Passive Voice). Finally, put the subject and verb *first* in the sentence since the subject and the main verb are the message of the sentence.

Use personal pronouns to make fewer mistakes with subject and verb agreement (see also Pronouns).
We (plural subject) *have decided* (plural main verb) *to change the policy.*

Writing *staff is* is strictly correct since *staff* is a collective noun and so staff is *singular.* Change the subject to a plural form if in doubt.
Staff members (plural subject) *are* (plural main verb) *free to decide for themselves.*

Use a singular pronoun with a singular expression. Alternatively, make the subject of the sentence plural.
*Everyone must clear **his or her** shelf by next week.*
*Team members must clear **their** shelves by next week.*

Writing tips for active and passive voice

Use the active voice. Use the passive voice only where appropriate. For example, use the passive voice when you do not know who performed an action. Alternatively, use the passive voice when the object is more important than the subject in the mind of the user.

Put the subject and main verb in the first position in the sentence. Keep the subject and main verb together. Separating the subject and main verb with extra information makes the subject and main verb difficult to identify.

Be aware of how voice influences your style and tone. Be equally aware of how voice influences the way in which you think.

Writing tips for conditional sentences

We used to consider starting a sentence with a conjunction as grammatically incorrect. Now we consider starting a sentence with a conjunction in formal business writing as an *inappropriate* style (see also Conjunctions).

Avoid starting a sentence with a conjunction by switching the two clauses of a conditional sentence. You will start your sentences with a clear subject and main verb also if you switch the action clause with the condition clause (see also Conjunctions).

Write *if the machine stops, push the red button* as *push the red button if the machine stops.*
(See also Imperative Mood).

3 Structuring information

Writing tips for paragraphs	Use a topic sentence for each paragraph in longer documents.
	Be consistent in your use of keywords even if you feel that you are repeating yourself. Too many synonyms can make speed reading your text difficult for your user.
	Keep your paragraphs to between three and six sentences. Have at least three paragraphs per page. Block your paragraphs and leave a space between each paragraph. Only left-justify your paragraphs.
	Use subheadings throughout your text.

Short cut grammar tips for apostrophes	You can test whether something belongs to someone or something else by changing the *structure* of a sentence.
	Change *the team's objectives* to *the objectives of the team*. In this case, *the objectives* clearly belong to *the team*. Consequently, write *team's* with an apostrophe.
	Change *the teams attend* to *the attend of the team*. In this case, *attend* is clearly a verb (see also Verbs). Consequently, do not write *teams* with an apostrophe since the word is plural.

Writing tips for punctuation	Use only essential punctuation in business writing. In other words, use punctuation only where punctuation will help your user to make sense of the information on the page.
	Write in simple and compound sentences (see also Sentences). Sentences made of only *one or two ideas* are easier for your user to process. Furthermore, shorter sentences require only essential punctuation.
	Avoid using contractions in *formal* business writing (see also Verbs). As a result, you will never be confused between *its* and *it's* if you avoid contracting the verb *is* to the pronoun *it* (see also Pronouns).
	Joining sentences with a semi-colon or a colon is a sophisticated use of punctuation. You can communicate your message with equal effect by joining your sentences with a conjunction such as *and* (see also Conjunctions). Only join your sentences with a semi-colon or a colon if that style will contribute to your user accepting your message.

Writing tips for style and tone

Be emotionally intelligent in your business writing. In other words, use an appropriate amount of emotion in your writing to make your message acceptable to your user.

Plan your style and tone before you start writing. Use a style and tone which is appropriate to your objective. Your objective is to make your user accept your message so that you can achieve your purpose.

Use plain English for texts which have a wide or undefined audience. Use plain English for multicultural or multilingual audiences. Use jargon and technical language where appropriate for specialised audiences.

Use metaphor only where metaphor will contribute to achieving your objectives.

Use an assertive tone in your business writing. In other words, acknowledge your own rights and the rights of others when you are writing.

Avoid generalisations. Use facts if references to *age*, *creed*, *culture*, *gender*, *race*, or *sexual orientation* are relevant to your message.

Use humour only when humour is appropriate to you achieving your objective. Avoid sarcasm and innuendo. Instead, be assertive. Use irony and euphemism only when irony and euphemism are appropriate to you achieving your objective.

Avoid hyperbole and understatement. Instead, use *facts*, *actions*, *suggestions*, *decisions*, and *time-scales*.

Control your direct message and you will control your indirect message. We send our direct message in words and we *imply* our indirect message as an overall impression.

Create a *positive* tone in your writing by avoiding negative statements and words. Use negative prefixes instead of the word *not* (see also Prefixes).

Avoid an *emphatic* tone in your writing. Avoid tautology; repetitive phrasal verbs; and emphatic adverbs such as *actually*.

Write in complete sentences. Keep your subject and main verb together. Furthermore, put the subject and the main verb in the *first* position in the sentence. Consequently, use the acive voice.

Use simple and compound sentences. In other words, limit your sentences to *one or two ideas*.

Avoid embedding phrases, clauses, and even other sentences into your main sentence. Avoid separating your subject and main verb.

Avoid contractions and phrasal verbs in formal business writing. Contractions and phrasal verbs are appropriate to informal or conversational texts.

Use verbs as verbs. In other words, avoid turning verbs into nouns through the process of nominalisation (see also Nouns and Verbs).

Use the relative pronoun *who* instead of the relative pronoun *that* when you refer to people.

Avoid ending sentences with a preposition in formal business writing.

Use only the punctuation which is essential to your user making sense of the information on the page.

F Solutions to exercises

Noun exercise answers

Essential exercise
answers Circle the nouns below. Remember to test the word with an article to
see if the word is a noun. Use *a*, *an*, or *the* in front of the word.

staff	sue	yours	**drive**	were
I	their	bad	**feel**	**cord**
send	**file**	see	**loss**	**cut**
speed	eat	long	could	extend
fast	**find**	it	you	**serve**
coach	**end**	now	**goods**	**post**
her	never	**talks**	red	**drag**
yet	**shares**	**might**	his	**plain**

Bridging exercise
answers Circle the nouns below. Remember to test the word with an article to see if the word is a noun. Use *a*, *an*, or *the* in front of the word.

in-tray	shortish	**orange**	**success**	urgent
smoking	**fraudster**	**finish**	**water**	**anger**
clever	consult	itself	wasn't	**panic**
programme	**letter**	**growing**	**pressure**	will be
hopeful	**audit**	over here	clearly	**return**
badly	**Europe**	**beauty**	unique	**defence**
order	**despair**	denote	**client**	**complaint**
myself	slower	seldom	put aside	**wanting**

Applied exercise
answers Circle the nouns below. Remember to test the word with an article to see if the word is a noun. Use *a*, *an*, or *the* in front of the word.

typically	**Wall Street**	beautiful	**company**	judgmental
Australia	**manager**	**Japanese**	relocate	**consultant**
sensitive	**denotation**	**enclosure**	selected	**eraser**
flawlessly	**United Kingdom**	anyway	**operations**	happier
salary	uncomfortable	**advisor**	**breakfast**	communicate
paper clip	**Americanese**	**employer**	necessary	inadvertently
secretary	hopelessly	**FTSE 100**	stupidly	capable
director	**conglomerate**	adamantly	**projection**	international

Personal pronoun exercise answers

Write the correct personal pronoun into the following sentences.

First person singular *I* own the book. The book belongs to **me**. No one may take **my** book. The book is **mine**. I bought the book for **myself**.	**Second person singular** *You* own the book. The book belongs to **you**. No one may take **your** book. The book is **yours**. You bought the book for **yourself**.
Third person singular masculine *He* owns the book. The book belongs to **him**. No one may take **his** book. The book is **his**. He bought the book for **himself**.	**Third person singular feminine** *She* owns the book. The book belongs to **her**. No one may take **her** book. The book is **hers**. She bought the book for **herself**.
Third person singular neutral *It* owns the book. The book belongs to **it**. No one may take **its** book. The book is **its**. It bought the book for **itself**.	**First person plural** *We* own the book. The book belongs to **us**. No one may take **our** book. The book is **ours**. We bought the book for **ourselves**.
Second person plural *You* own the book. The book belongs to **you**. No one may take **your** book. The book is **yours**. You bought the book for **yourselves**.	**Third person plural** *They* own the book. The book belongs to **them**. No one may take **their** book. The book is **theirs**. They bought the book for **themselves**.

Applied exercise
answers

Complete the following table of personal pronouns.

Person	Subject pronoun	Object pronoun	Possessive pronoun	Genitive pronoun	Reflexive pronoun
First Person Singular:	I	**me**	**my**	mine	**myself**
Second Person Singular:	**you**	**you**	your	**yours**	yourself
Third Person Singular (Masculine):	**he**	him	**his**	his	**himself**
Third Person Singular (Feminine):	she	**her**	**her**	hers	**herself**
Third Person Singular (Neutral):	**it**	**it**	its	**its**	itself
First Person Plural:	**we**	**us**	**our**	ours	**ourselves**
Second Person Plural:	**you**	you	**your**	**yours**	**yourselves**
Third Person Plural:	they	**them**	**their**	**theirs**	**themselves**

Adjective exercise answers

Circle the adjectives below. Remember to test the word to see if it is an adjective by putting the word in front of a noun. Remember also to test the word by putting the word in the position of the predicate of the sentence. Use a form such as "the object is (word)".

you	start	**short**	**down**	it's
would	book	me	dial	lunch
long	**that**	type	do	print
ours	sue	chair	**yours**	**his**
still	**staple**	switch	**there**	should
meet	pay	**this**	phone	**your**
slow	**clean**	freeze	**fast**	doubt
plan	hope	**weak**	**bound**	press

Bridging exercise answers

Circle the adjectives below. Remember to test the word to see if it is an adjective by putting the word in front of a noun. Remember also to test the word by putting the word in the position of the predicate of the sentence. Use a form such as "the object is (word)".

copy	**friendly**	**ugly**	**over there**	**anxious**
themselves	**smaller**	dinner	author	weren't
faster	stapler	**eager**	habit	**hopeful**
enclose	**rising**	**frowning**	customs	**crushing**
yellow	save in	**major**	denial	**icy**
contact	suspend	slowly	**urgent**	neatly
England	laptop	herself	issues	won't
failure	**spiral**	button	confirm	declare

Applied exercise answers

Circle the adjectives below. Remember to test the word to see if it is an adjective by putting the word in front of a noun. Remember also to test the word by putting the word in the position of the predicate of the sentence. Use a form such as "the object is (word)".

unavoidably	commencement	inexpressibly	**immediate**	receptionist
suspension	management	division	cleverly	**fraudulent**
computer	establish	**substantial**	Canada	West Indies
touchy-feely	**interpersonal**	**stationary**	reception	immediately
establishment	connotation	terminate	engineer	**European**
police officer	associate	mistakenly	nevertheless	**multinational**
prejudiced	New Zealand	redundancy	purchasing	**erroneous**
corroborate	reify	**well-illustrated**	remunerate	exemplify

Preposition exercise answers

Complete the following word combinations by adding a preposition.

thanks **to**	apart **from**	further **to**
save **for**	instead **of**	owing **to**
short **of**	along **with**	outside **of**
down **to**	away **from**	prior **to**
due **to**	because **of**	except **for**
care **of**	subject **to**	as well **as**

Complete the following word combinations by adding a preposition.

by means **of**	in case **of**	relative **to**
by way **of**	in terms **of**	as opposed **to**
in lieu **of**	according **to**	in contrast **with**
in line **with**	contrary **to**	in contrast **to**
in spite **of**	together **with**	in favour **of**
on top **of**	regardless **of**	in keeping **with**

Complete the following word combinations by adding a preposition.

accompanied **by**	on behalf **of**	in the case **of**
irrespective **of**	with respect **to**	in the course **of**
subsequent **to**	with regard **to**	in the line **of**
in regard **to**	in addition **to**	on the grounds **of**
in respect **of**	in common **with**	in conjunction **with**
in response **to**	with reference **to**	in connection **with**
in return **for**	as a result **of**	in accordance **with**
on account **of**	on the part **of**	in comparison **with**

Verb exercise answers

Circle the verbs below. Remember to use the preposition *to* if you want to test whether the word is a verb. The word is a verb if we can *perform* the word as an action.

them	**coach**	blue	here	**shall**
chair	**fold**	her	**fast**	small
black	day	**hope**	**green**	**will**
you	up	your	**fax**	our
fear	**mine**	**post**	its	**be**
file	tall	any	week	**buy**
lunch	**get**	**sit**	**long**	he
click	door	**clip**	glass	**need**

Circle the verbs below. Remember to use the preposition *to* if you want to test whether the word is a verb. The word is a verb if we can *perform* the word as an action.

audit	lawyer	**copy**	notebook	yourselves
file away	**advise**	**look after**	minor	**boycott**
despatch	himself	**commence**	advice	**frustrate**
costings	smiling	anxious	quickly	**present**
fearful	**exchange**	**index**	**perceive**	internal
despair	mostly	**delay**	hostile	politely
program	larger	flawless	sliding	reactive
sanctions	**receive**	anxiety	sharpener	**expect**

Applied exercise answers Circle the verbs below. Remember to use the preposition *to* if you want to test whether the word is a verb. The word is a verb if we can *perform* the word as an action.

barrister	personal	speedily	**administrate**	consequently
stock market	American	**envelope**	**authorise**	necessity
hopefully	unavoidable	frequently	correctly	subsequently
send away for	administrator	**pigeon hole**	mistaken	incompetent
Falkland Islands	pathetically	**objectify**	appraisal	inadvertent
delegate	attractive	pathetic	get-together	South Africa
chairperson	United States	**aggravate**	**telephone**	minimal
accountant	disinterested	emergency	programme	fatality

Adverb exercise answers

Essential exercise answers Circle the adverbs below. Remember that adverbs usually end in the suffix *-ly* but some adverbs are exceptions. Test the word by relating the word to a verb. An adverb will indicate *when*, *where*, or *how* we perform an action.

my	desk	keep	**now**	**weekly**
here	theirs	**then**	hers	we
yearly	him	team	**daily**	**ever**
fax	**quickly**	**today**	dine	may
big	book	cope	call	**monthly**
loosely	you	its	they	won't
white	**well**	good	**shortly**	**there**
stamp	ring	am	bind	was

Bridging exercise answers

Circle the adverbs below. Remember that adverbs usually end in the suffix -*ly* but some adverbs are exceptions. Test the word by relating the word to a verb. An adverb will indicate *when*, *where*, or *how* we perform an action.

ourselves	**often**	yourself	falling	**before**
lately	concede	**perfectly**	decide	Hong Kong
purchase	keyboard	afraid	**only**	**caringly**
purple	**mostly**	section	decade	customer
send out	call up	**deeply**	bigger	**externally**
happily	season	proof-read	paper	holdings
enjoy	**quicker**	touchy	out-tray	extension
represent	confident	**willingly**	photograph	**slightly**

Applied exercise answers

Circle the adverbs below. Remember that adverbs usually end in the suffix -*ly* but some adverbs are exceptions. Test the word by relating the word to a verb. An adverb will indicate *when*, *where*, or *how* we perform an action.

communication	**abundantly**	journalese	**usually**	courier
America	prejudice	annual	directorship	**exceptionally**
tomorrow	**please**	**fearfully**	stationery	competent
employee	Zimbabwe	relocation	counterfeit	**distantly**
perceptively	**decidedly**	**naturally**	administration	the largest
specialist	take-over	write away for	every	**effectively**
decisively	filing cabinet	**authoritatively**	English	India
Dow Jones Index	redistribution	melancholy	**operationally**	rationalise

General sentence exercise answers

Change the following groups of words into complete sentences if necessary. Some of the following are suggested answers only.

1. I (**subject**) refer (**main verb**) to your letter of 8 January 2001.

2. [I (**subject**)] thank (**main verb**) you for your prompt reply.

3. We (**subject**) stock (**main verb**) stationary including paper, envelopes, and stamps.

4. [I (**subject**)] thank (**main verb**) you in advance.

5. [You (**subject**) must (**modal verb**)] lift (**infinitive verb**) the cover and adjust (**infinitive verb**) the dial.

6. You (**subject**) may (**modal verb**) not smoke (**infinitive verb**).

7. Rising costs (**subject**) have forced (**main verb**) the business to close.

8. The team (**subject**) consists (**main verb**) of specialists and support staff.

9. The team (**subject**) has done (**main verb**) well.

10. The end-of-year results (**subject**) show (**main verb**) a fall in profits. You (**subject**) will find (**main verb**) a full explanation below.

Tense exercise answers

Initial tense
exercise answers

Conjugate the auxiliary verb *to be* in the simple tense.

Person	Past	Present	Future
I	*was*	*am*	*will be*
You	**were**	**are**	**will be**
He/she/it	**was**	**is**	**will be**
We	**were**	**are**	**will be**
You	**were**	**are**	**will be**
They	**were**	**are**	**will be**

Conjugate the auxiliary verb *to be* in the continuous tense.

Person	Past	Present	Future
I	*was being*	*am being*	*will be being*
You	**were being**	**are being**	**will be being**
He/she/it	**was being**	**is being**	**will be being**
We	**were being**	**are being**	**will be being**
You	**were being**	**are being**	**will be being**
They	**were being**	**are being**	**will be being**

Conjugate the auxiliary verb *to do* in the simple tense.

Person	Past	Present	Future
I	*did*	*do*	*will do*
You	**did**	**do**	**will do**
He/she/it	**did**	**does**	**will do**
We	**did**	**do**	**will do**
You	**did**	**do**	**will do**
They	**did**	**do**	**will do**

Conjugate the auxiliary verb *to do* in the continuous tense.

Person	Past	Present	Future
I	*was doing*	*am doing*	*will be doing*
You	**were doing**	**are doing**	**will be doing**
He/she/it	**was doing**	**is doing**	**will be doing**
We	**were doing**	**are doing**	**will be doing**
You	**were doing**	**are doing**	**will be doing**
They	**were doing**	**are doing**	**will be doing**

Conjugate the auxiliary verb *to have* in the simple tense.

Person	Past	Present	Future
I	*had*	*have*	*will have*
You	**had**	**have**	**will have**
He/she/it	**had**	**has**	**will have**
We	**had**	**have**	**will have**
You	**had**	**have**	**will have**
They	**had**	**have**	**will have**

Conjugate the auxiliary verb *to have* in the continuous tense.

Person	Past	Present	Future
I	*was having*	*am having*	*will be having*
You	**were having**	**are having**	**will be having**
He/she/it	**was having**	**is having**	**will be having**
We	**were having**	**are having**	**will be having**
You	**were having**	**are having**	**will be having**
They	**were having**	**are having**	**will be having**

Rewrite the following sentences so that the verbs are in the correct tense. Remember that a sentence can contain more than one verb. However, one of those verbs must be a main verb. The main verb of a sentence tells us two things: *what* happened and *when* that action happened. In other words, a main verb must have a tense. All subsequent verbs will be in the infinitive tense.

1. Denise *will book* (**future simple**) the tickets tomorrow.

2. The courier *delivered* (**past simple**) the package last week.

3. The supplier *delivers* (**present simple**) the groceries every day at 10am.

4. I *have enclosed* (**present perfect**) a brochure and an order form for you *to consider* (**infinitive**).

5. We *sent* (**past simple**) the package last week but nothing *has arrived* (**present perfect**) yet.

6. We *sent* (**past simple**) the new package last week but nothing *arrived* (**past simple**) until yesterday.

7. I *faxed* (**past simple**) joining instructions last week for you *to look at* (**infinitive phrasal verb**) before you *leave* (**present simple**) next Tuesday.

8. I *was thinking* (**past continuous**) about you when you *called* (**past simple**) yesterday because I *had not been able* (**past perfect**) *to find* (**infinitive**) your order form.

Rewrite the following sentences so that the verbs are in the correct tense. Remember that a sentence can contain more than one verb. However, one of those verbs must be a main verb. The main verb of a sentence tells us two things: *what* happened and *when* that action happened. In other words, a main verb must have a tense. All subsequent verbs will be in the infinitive tense.

9. We *have visited* (**present perfect**) the clients twice but the clients *have not decided* (**present perfect**) yet whether *to use* (**infinitive**) our services.

10. You *must* (**modal**) *cancel* (**infinitive**) all tickets within at least fourteen working days from the date of issue if you *want* (**present simple**) a refund.

11. The magazine *printed* (**past simple**) the article a fortnight ago while he *was travelling* (**past continuous**) abroad. Consequently, he *has not seen* (**present perfect**) nor *read* (**present perfect**) anything yet.

12. You *must* (**modal**) *save* (**infinitive**) the material while you *are working* (**present continuous**) still on the file. Otherwise, you *will lose* (**future simple**) all the work you *have completed* (**present perfect**) if the power *fails* (**present simple**) unexpectedly.

13. We *must* (**modal**) *not underestimate* (**infinitive**) the difficulty of this situation. We *cannot* (**modal**) *assume* (**infinitive**) that our competitors *will not grasp* (**future simple**) the opportunity if they *come* (**present simple**) *to hear* (**infinitive**) of anything.

14. We *expected* (**past simple**) the client *to call* (**infinitive**) yesterday. However, the client *has not called* (**present perfect**) and we *have been unable* (**present perfect**) *to reach* (**infinitive**) him since then. In the meantime, we *will continue* (**future simple**) to work on the proposal.

15. We *had* (**past simple**) *to remove* (**infinitive**) the walls before we *could* (**modal**) *begin* (**infinitive**) constructing the foundations. In fact, we *are laying* (**present continuous**) still the foundations and we *do not expect* (**present simple**) *to finish* (**infinitive**) until next month.

16. The company *had been considering* (**past perfect continuous**) the option of recruiting new staff before the merger *occurred* (**past simple**) last year. However, we now *have decided* (**present perfect**) instead *to decrease* (**infinitive**) our production for the time being as this tactic *will be* (**future simple**) more cost effective.

Applied exercise answers

Rewrite the following sentences so that the verbs are in the correct tense. Remember that a sentence can contain more than one verb. However, one of those verbs must be a main verb. The main verb of a sentence tells us two things: *what* happened and *when* that action happened. In other words, a main verb must have a tense. All subsequent verbs will be in the infinitive tense.

17. Abdul *was* (**past simple**) responsible for managing over twenty members of staff and *created* (**past simple**) a 20% increase in production while he *was working* (**past continuous**) for this section. We *were thinking* (**past continuous**) of promoting him again when he *announced* (**past simple**) his decision *to leave* (**infinitive**).

18. The department *will have been using* (**future perfect continuous**) the current system for four years by the time that the new system *comes* (**present simple**) into place next year. Unfortunately, we *had bought* (**past perfect**) the new system before we *learnt* (**past simple**) that we *will be moving* (**past continuous**) to a larger location in the city next autumn.

19. We *have been* (**present perfect**) concerned over the last four months about your attendance at work. We *would* (**modal**) *like* (**infinitive**) *to speak* (**infinitive**) to you about this situation before the end of the month. I *need* (**present simple**) *to arrange* (**infinitive**) a time when we *can* (**modal**) *meet* (**infinitive**) *to discuss* (**infinitive**) this matter in detail.

20. A multinational recently *acquired* (**past simple**) the company while the company *was undergoing* (**past continuous**) still major re-engineering. The acquisition *caused* (**past simple**) six key members of staff *to defect* (**infinitive**) to rival companies. Three other key members *have indicated* (**present perfect**) that they *will be leaving* (**future continuous**) in the near future.

21. The company *has seen* (**present perfect**) a significant increase in production over the last year but as we *look* (**present simple**) to the coming year, we *expect* (**present simple**) the increase *to fall* (**infinitive**) slightly. We *have been developing* (**present perfect continuous**) a new strategy in the last two months and we *will implement* (**future simple**) this strategy in the first quarter next year.

22. We *have put* (**present perfect**) always the quality of our production first but in future we *will be thinking* (**future continuous**) also of marketing more aggressively. We *hope* (**present simple**) *to increase* (**infinitive**) our sales potential this way. We *will have been working* (**future perfect continuous**) with the new agency for at least a year before we *will see* (**future simple**) a measurable difference in our sales.

23. The trader *invested* (**past simple**) in an international company without the prior permission of the board. As a result, we *were unable* (**past simple**) *to recover* (**infinitive**) the money after the company *had collapsed* (**past perfect**). We *need* (**present simple**) *to establish* (**infinitive**) clear procedures which *will prevent* (**future simple**) this from happening in future although the amount of money *was* (**past simple**) small.

24. The company's two new products *will be entering* (**future continuous**) production next month and we *expect* (**present simple**) *to be* (**infinitive**) in the marketplace before the end of the year. Nevertheless, we *cannot* (**modal**) *stress* (**infinitive**) enough the importance of continuing *to promote* (**infinitive**) our existing production line. Furthermore, we *need* (**present simple**) *to conduct* (**infinitive**) this promotion with the same amount of vigour as we *have* (**present perfect** – abbreviated from *have conducted*) in the past.

Subject and verb agreement exercise answers

Consider the agreement between the subject and the main verb in the following sentences. Rewrite the sentences if the subject and the main verb disagree. In each case, change the main verb to agree with the subject.

1. The *team* (singular **subject**) *is meeting* (singular **main verb**) next week.

2. The *council* (singular **subject**) *meets* (singular **main verb**) today in Room 509.

3. The *media* (singular **subject**) *is discussing* (singular **main verb**) a new policy.

   Media is strictly plural since the word is the plural form of the Latin word *medium*. However, we now tend to treat most of our words in English as words in their own right. Consequently, we tend to treat *media* as singular. We can classify *media* as a collective noun which refers to all our forms of mass communication and so we treat the word as singular.

4. The *premises* (plural **subject**) *close* (plural **main verb**) at 9.00pm on weeknights.

5. The *data* (singular **subject**) *is* (singular **main verb**) stored on the hard drive of the computer.

   Data is strictly plural since the word is the plural form of the Latin word *datum*. However, we now tend to treat most of our words in English as words in their own right. Consequently, we tend to treat *data* as singular. We can classify *data* as a collective noun which refers to a mass of information and so we treat the word as singular.

6. *Staff* (singular **subject**) *is* (singular **main verb**) responsible for the maintenance of the storeroom.

7. We sent a memo explaining how the *department* (singular **subject**) *is* (singular **main verb**) accountable for the new policy.

8. The *support staff* (singular **subject**) *feels* (singular **main verb**) that *management* (singular **subject**) *does* (singular **main verb**) *not communicate* everything which *support staff* (singular **subject**) *needs* (singular **main verb**) to know.

Bridging exercise answers Consider the agreement between the subject and the main verb in the following sentences. Rewrite the sentences if the subject and the main verb disagree. In each case, change the main verb to agree with the subject.

9. We introduced a policy of continuous maintenance in the department a year ago. Consequently, *everyone* (singular **subject**) of us now *is doing* (singular **main verb**) his or her share.

10. The new system saves time and money for the department. As a result, *none* (singular **subject**) of us *has* (singular **main verb**) the right of not participating since we all benefit from the new system.

11. The department meeting takes place on Wednesday at 10.30am. *Either Sunil or Mary* (singular **subject**) *are presenting* (singular **main verb**) the team's monthly report. A copy of the report will be available tomorrow.

12. A *number* (singular **subject**) of changes *has* (singular **main verb**) occurred in the section since the merger. Many people have seen their jobs alter and *management* (singular **subject**) *has* (singular **main verb**) to create the structures to facilitate these changes.

13. A *series* (singular **subject**) of thefts *has* (singular **main verb**) occurred in the building and a *number* (singular **subject**) of laptops *has* (singular **main verb**) gone missing. However, neither *management* (singular **subject**) nor the relevant *consultants* (plural **subject**) *feel* (plural **main verb**) that an independent investigation is necessary.

14. The *Board* (singular **subject**) of Directors *is meeting* (singular **main verb**) in London on Thursday morning. Consequently, the conference rooms on the third floor will be unavailable. Furthermore, the *Directors* (plural **subject**) *are going* (plural **main verb**) to have lunch on the terrace from 12.00pm.

15. We are expanding our client base as part of our new drive to increase our profit margin. The *team* (singular **subject**) *has* (singular **subject**) compiled a proposal which will outline our new strategy. *Either Patricia, the team leader, or the consulting team* (singular **subject**) *is presenting* (singular **subject**) the new document.

16. The main *objectives* (plural **subject**) of the quarterly report *are* (plural **main verb**) to outline the key changes. We need to implement these changes to the production process to improve both speed and quality. However, *none* (singular **subject**) of the report's three recommendations *is* (singular **main verb**) suitable for our purposes.

Applied exercise answers

Consider the agreement between the subject and the main verb in the following sentences. Rewrite the sentences if the subject and the main verb disagree. In each case, change the main verb to agree with the subject.

17. A large *portion* (singular **subject**) of the profits *has* (singular **main verb**) disappeared as a result of our new staff recruitment. The *recruitment* (singular **subject**) of new staff members *means* (singular **main verb**) that our overheads have risen without us generating new income. The *appendices* (plural **subject**) *contain* (plural **main verb**) a full breakdown on the cost of recruitment.

18. The *media* (singular **subject**) *has leaked* (singular **main verb**) information contained in a report which the *company* (singular **subject**) *has* not *published* (singular **main verb**) yet. *Senior management* (singular **subject**) *meets* (singular **main verb**) this afternoon to discuss the legal implications of the leak. The *agenda* (singular **subject**) *covers* (singular **main verb**) a discussion on whether or not the *media* (singular **subject**) *is* (plural **main verb**) legally responsible for the leak.

    Agenda is strictly plural since the word is the plural form of the Latin word *agendum*. However, we now tend to treat most of our words in English as words in their own right. Consequently, we tend to treat *agenda* as singular. We can classify *agenda* as a collective noun which refers to a group of items for discussion and so we treat the word as singular. See Answer 3 for an explanation of *media*.

19. The *group* (singular **subject**) <u>*has*</u> *decided* (singular **main verb**) to change the focus of the project. Initially, the project focused on the marketing plan for the company's two new products. However, the *Senior Management Team* (singular **subject**) <u>*has*</u> *decided* (singular **main verb**) to delay the launch of both products. Consequently, the *group* (singular **subject**) <u>*do*</u> (singular **main verb**) *not have* a specific project on which to focus at the moment.

---

20. The first *floor* (singular **subject**) <u>*has*</u> (singular **main verb**) to evacuate the building by taking the following route. Staff must descend by the rear stairway and exit through the rear entrance. Furthermore, the second *floor* (singular **subject**) <u>*has*</u> (singular **main verb**) to evacuate the building in a similar fashion. However, the third *floor* (singular **subject**) <u>*has*</u> (singular **main verb**) to descend the front stairway and exit the building through the main entrance.

---

21. *Twenty-five per cent* (singular **subject**) of profits <u>*has*</u> *fallen* (singular **main verb**) in the last quarter. The finance *department* (singular **subject**) <u>*has*</u> *compiled* (singular **main verb**) a report which outlines the speculation over the sudden decrease. Nevertheless, the report also indicates that *10%* (singular **subject**) of costs also <u>*has*</u> *fallen* (singular **main verb**). Consequently, the *fall* (singular **subject**) in profits <u>*is*</u> (singular **main verb**) not as threatening as the initial *figures* (plural **subject**) in the report <u>*suggest*</u> (plural **main verb**).

---

22. The *budget* (singular **subject**) of the marketing team <u>*has*</u> *escalated* (singular **main verb**) in the last six months. Consequently, the profit *margin* (singular **subject**) of the team <u>*has*</u> *lessened* (singular **main verb**) proportionately. *Management* (singular **subject**) <u>*is*</u> (singular **main verb**) concerned about the situation and about where the budget may go in future. As a result, *management* (singular **subject**) <u>*has*</u> *asked* (singular **main verb**) the team to provide suggestions to reduce the costs of production.

23. The *department* (singular **subject**) *has cancelled* (singular **main verb**) the three-day workshop for catering staff. Four members of the human resources department arranged the workshop to help catering staff. The main *objectives* (plural **subject**) of the workshop *were* (plural **main verb**) to develop new systems of communication for internal customers. However, the *demands* (plural **subject**) of the autumn season on the kitchen *mean* (plural **main verb**) that *none* (singular **subject**) of the staff *is* (singular **main verb**) available to attend.

---

24. The key *goals* (plural **subject**) of the Financial Support Team *are* (plural **main verb**) outlined in the new systems proposal. The *department* (singular **subject**) *expects* (singular **main verb**) all members of the team to attend a briefing on the new document by the end of the month. Furthermore, the *department* (singular **subject**) *invites* (singular **subject**) members of the team to submit their questions or objections before the briefing. The *department* (singular **subject**) *is preparing* (singular **subject**) currently a questionnaire to circulate to the team.

Active and passive voice exercise answers

Change the following sentences into the active voice if the sentences are in the passive voice. Leave the sentences unchanged if the sentences are in the active voice.

1. Active voice
   John (**subject**) called (**main verb**) a meeting (**object**).

2. Passive voice
   The letter (**object**) was typed (**main verb**) by Lee (**subject**).

   Active voice
   Lee (**subject**) typed (**main verb**) thc letter (**object**).

3. Passive voice
   The database (**object**) was updated (**main verb**) yesterday by Jane (**subject**).

   Active voice
   Jane (**subject**) updated (**main verb**) the database (**object**) yesterday.

4. Active voice
   Carol (**subject**) had prepared (**main verb**) the presentation (**object**) weeks before the event.

5. Active voice
   She (**subject**) switched (**main verb** - phrasal verb with preposition *off*) the computer (**object**) off before she (**subject**) left (**main verb**) the office (**object**) last night.

6. Passive voice
   The customer (**object**) who complained about the product (**identifying relative clause**) was sent (**main verb**) a full refund.

   Active voice
   We (**subject**) sent (**main verb**) the customer (**object**) who complained about the product (**identifying relative clause**) a full refund.

7. Passive voice
   The team (**object**) has been given (**main verb**) a full report on the changes to be made (**infinitive verb**) to the department.

   Active voice
   We (**subject**) have given (**main verb**) the team (**object**) a full report on the changes we (**subject**) will make (**main verb**) to the department.

   ---

8. Passive voice
   A series (**object**) of proposals has been submitted (**main verb**) to the committee. A decision (**object**) will be made (**main verb**) at the next meeting.

   Active voice
   We (**subject**) have submitted (**main verb**) a series (**object**) of proposals to the committee. The committee (**subject**) will make (**main verb**) a decision (**object**) at the next meeting.

Bridging exercise answers

Change the following sentences into the active voice if the sentences are in the passive voice. Leave the sentences unchanged if the sentences are in the active voice.

9. Passive voice
   The post (**object**) was delivered (**main verb**) this morning to reception. However, the package (**object**) which we were expecting (identifying relative cause) had not been sent (**main verb**) with the delivery.

   Active voice (suggested answer)
   The postman (**subject**) delivered (**main verb**) the post (**object**) this morning to reception. However, the client (**subject**) had not sent (**main verb**) the package (**object**) which we were expecting with the delivery.

10. Active and passive voice
The room (**object**) will be cleaned (**main verb**) when we (**subject**) leave (**main verb**). Nevertheless, those attending (**object**) the seminar are expected (**main verb**) to clear any waste before leaving.

Active voice (suggested answer)
The cleaner (**subject**) will clean (**main verb**) the room (**object**) when we (**subject**) leave (**main verb**). Nevertheless, we (**subject**) expect (**main verb**) those attending (**object**) the seminar to clear any waste before leaving.

11. Passive voice
We (**object**) were met (**main verb**) at the reception and taken (**main verb**) upstairs. However, we (**object**) were left (**main verb**) to wait in a small room without refreshments for nearly half-an-hour.

Active voice (suggested answer)
Our host (**subject**) met (**main verb**) us (**object**) at the reception and took (**main verb**) us (**object**) upstairs. However, our host (**subject**) left (**main verb**) us (**object**) to wait in a small room without refreshments for nearly half-an-hour.

(Note how the subject pronoun *we* in the passive voice changes to the object pronoun *us* in the active voice [see also Pronouns]).

12. Active and passive voice
He (**subject**) reported (**main verb**) the mistake (**object**) but nothing (**object**) was done (**main verb**). As a result, an investigation (**object**) into the system is awaited (**main verb**) and a full report (**object**) has been commissioned (**main verb**).

Active voice
He (**subject**) reported (**main verb**) the mistake (**object**) but no one (**subject**) did (**main verb**) anything (**object**). As a result, we (**subject**) await (**main verb**) an investigation (**object**) into the system and we (**subject**) have commissioned (**main verb**) a full report (**object**).

13. Active and passive voice
    Rachel (**subject**) was (**main verb**) unhappy about the way Martin (**subject**) had spoken (**main verb**) to her (**object**) at the meeting. Nevertheless, an agreement (**object**) was made (**main verb**) to finish the project together.

    Rachel (**subject**) was (**main intransitive verb**) unhappy about the way Martin (**subject**) had spoken (**main verb**) to her (**object**) at the meeting. Nevertheless, Rachel and Martin (**subject**) made (**main verb**) an agreement (**object**) to finish the project together.

    (*To be* is an intransitive verb which cannot take an object; consequently, we cannot write the first sentence in the passive voice [see also verbs].)

14. Active and passive voice
    The supplies (**object**) have been delivered (**main verb**) consistently behind schedule in the last month. Furthermore, the quality (**subject**) of the products has not been (**main intransitive verb**) to standard.

    Active voice
    They (**subject**) have delivered (**main verb**) the supplies (**object**) consistently behind schedule in the last month. Furthermore, the quality (**subject**) of the products has not been (**main intransitive verb**) to standard.

15. Passive voice
    The structure (**object**) of the book has been reworked (**main verb**) extensively since the first draft. However, no clearance (**object**) has been given (**main verb**) for the publication of the material.

    Active voice
    The author (**subject**) has reworked (**main verb**) the structure (**object**) of the book extensively since the first draft. However, the author (**subject**) has given (**main verb**) no clearance (**object**) for the publication of the material.

16. Passive voice

The costs (**object**) have been calculated (**main verb**) and approval (**object**) for the project is being sought (**main verb**) currently. Approval (**object**) for the figures is expected (**main verb**) from the committee by the end of the month.

Active voice

We (**subject**) have calculated (**main verb**) the costs (**object**) and we (**subject**) are seeking (**main verb**) approval currently for the project. We (**subject**) expect (**main verb**) approval (**object**) from the committee for the figures by the end of the month.

Applied exercise answers Change the following sentences into the active voice if the sentences are in the passive voice. Leave the sentences unchanged if the sentences are in the active voice.

17. Passive voice

No applications (**object**) will be considered (**main verb**) by the Board from now on unless those applications (**object**) are submitted (**main verb**) in writing before the end of the year.

Active voice

The Board (**subject**) will not consider (**main verb**) applications (**object**) from now on unless you (**subject**) submit (**main verb**) those applications (**object**) in writing before the end of the year.

18. Passive voice

The computers (**object**) must be kept (**main verb**) clean of all food and drink. In the past, the equipment (**object**) has been damaged (**main verb**) due to carelessness and indifference.

Active voice

[You (**subject**) must] keep (**main verb**) the computers (**object**) clean of all food and drink. In the past, people (**subject**) have damaged (**main verb**) the equipment (**object**) due to carelessness and indifference.

19. Active voice
Fortunately, the figures (**subject**) for January show (**main verb**) an increase in income; however, the figures (**subject**) show (**main verb**) also a proportional increase in expenses so we (**subject**) have (**main verb**) no measurable difference in profit.

---

20. Passive voice
The workload (**object**) is expected (**main verb**) to increase in the coming months. Consequently, members (**subject**) of the team will have to (**main verb**) alternate shifts in order to manage the new pressures in a way which best suits our needs.

Active voice
We (**subject**) expect (**main verb**) the workload (**object**) to increase in the coming months. Consequently, members (**subject**) of the team will have to (**main verb**) alternate shifts in order to manage the new pressures in a way which best suits our needs

---

21. Passive voice
Profits (**object**) have been inflated (**main verb**) in the last quarter due to the recent merger. A full report (**object**) has been compiled (**main verb**) and the Board (**object**) has been briefed (**main verb**) on the implications. However, no new developments (**object**) are anticipated (**main verb**) in the coming months.

Active voice
The recent merger (**subject**) has inflated (**main verb**) profits (**object**) in the last quarter. We (**subject**) have compiled (**main verb**) a full report (**object**) and we (**subject**) have briefed (**main verb**) the Board (**object**) on the implications. However, we (**subject**) anticipate (**main verb**) no new developments (**object**) in the coming months.

22. Active and passive voice
The current change (**subject**) in administration has created (**main verb**) two new positions (**object**) which will have to be filled (**main verb**) before the end of June. Production (**object**) is needed (**main verb**) urgently to run efficiently as the system (**object**) has been scheduled (**main verb**) for redesign next year. Consequently, further delays (**object**) are expected (**main verb**).

Active voice
The current change (**subject**) in administration has created (**main verb**) two new positions. We (**subject**) will have to fill (**main verb**) these positions (**object**) before the end of June. We (**subject**) urgently need (**main verb**) production (**subject**) to run efficiently as we (**subject**) have scheduled (**main verb**) the system (**object**) for redesign next year. Consequently, we (**subject**) expect (**main verb**) further delays (**object**).

23. Passive and active voice
The measurements (**object**) have been taken (**main verb**) on your house. Nevertheless, the new landing (**object**) will not be able to be installed (**main verb**) until the carpet (**object**) is removed completely (**main verb**) from the lounge area below. Damage (**object**) has been incurred (**main verb**) in the past and removal (**subject**) will prevent (**main verb**) that damage (**object**) from happening again.

Active voice
We (**subject**) have taken (**main verb**) the measurements (**object**) on your house. Nevertheless, we (**subject**) will not be able to install (**main verb**) the new landing until we (**subject**) completely remove (**main verb**) the carpet (**object**) from the lounge area below. We (**subject**) have damaged (**main verb**) carpets (**object**) in the past and removal (**subject**) will prevent (**main verb**) that damage (**object**) from happening again.

24. Passive voice
    The construction (**object**) of the warehouse has been completed (**main verb**). The arrival (**object**) of stock is expected (**main verb**) to begin in the next few weeks according to the instructions of the company. However, the company (**object**) is warned (**main verb**) that until the roof (**object**) has been checked (**main verb**) completely, no guarantees (**object**) can be given (**main verb**) as to the safety of the warehouse.

    Active voice
    We (**subject**) have completed (**main verb**) the construction (**object**) of the warehouse. We (**subject**) expect (**main verb**) the stock (**object**) to begin arriving in the next few weeks according to the instructions of the company. However, we (**subject**) warn (**main verb**) the company (**object**) that we (**subject**) can give (**main verb**) no guarantees (**object**) as to the safety of the warehouse until we (**subject**) have checked (**main verb**) the roof (**object**) completely.

Direct and indirect speech exercise answers

Essential exercise answers

Change the following transcripts into indirect speech.

1. Samantha agreed.

2. Peter apologised for being late.

3. Tony asked Julia what she thought.

4. Leigh pointed out that their customers were complaining about their forms.

5. Colin asked whether anyone realised how the committee would respond when they heard.

6. Franco felt that the group had not listened to his point of view because people had been trying to meet their own needs.

Change the following transcripts into indirect speech.

7. The Officer confirmed that the accident had happened at two o' clock in the morning. Then the Officer asked why no one had called the police immediately.

8. Mark asked whether the audience could leave their questions until he had finished the presentation. He said that he found interruptions distracting which caused him to forget key pieces of information.

9. The chairperson said that they would meet again the following week if everyone was free on that Monday. The chairperson confirmed that everyone could attend on that day and then agreed to circulate the agenda that Friday.

10. She said that what they had seen there that day showed how effectively the team had worked in the previous six months. She added that the team had increased profits by 15% and had decreased costs by 5%.

11. He said that they had had four comments that in particular had been interesting. He asked if he should list the comments. The comments were that the venue was too small; the lunch had been inadequate; the room had had no air conditioning; and the presentation had been too long.

12. Barbara said that the truck had rolled on the highway at four o' clock that morning. She added that no one had been killed in the accident. However, the driver had been badly injured and was in intensive care. The co-driver had been unhurt but was in a state of shock.

Change the following transcripts into indirect speech.

13. Jennifer asked Mike whether he had had any new ideas about the project during the previous weekend. She added that Mike had seemed particularly inspired the week before about the work. She thought that some of the ideas which Mike had had would work brilliantly. She invited Mike to share those ideas with the group.

14. Reshna said that they needed to change the culture of the organisation if they were going to see any long-term results. She added that they would achieve little if they asked people to behave differently without giving those people the opportunity to change in the workplace. She pointed out that they would be sending a mixed message to the staff.

15. Richard said that over the next few months they would see a steady increase in costs as they recruited more staff. They would be inducting staff first before the staff started work about three months from then. Richard added that they needed everyone to be clear that the increase was a short-term effect. He pointed out that they expected to see an increase in production when the new staff members had found their feet.

16. Anne said that they were not sure yet how to put the system into place. They had thought of asking managers to check that people had completed the self-assessment during their one-to-ones. However, that idea put an extra burden on the managers who already had enough to do. Anne added that they had been hoping for more ideas from the group and she invited people to share their suggestions

17. Jousef said that their service users expected more attention now. They had to consider what the users wanted first before they made any changes to their services. They could not make decisions without asking first the people they were supposed to be helping. Jousef suggested that they do one of two things. They could establish either a focus group to discover what their users wanted or that they could compile a questionnaire to discover people's views.

18. Henry welcomed everyone to the meeting. Then Henry introduced John who presented the first item.

Paragraph exercise answers

Divide the following text into paragraphs. Remember that each paragraph should begin with a topic sentence. Remember also that no paragraph should explore more than one topic.

Start by finding and underlining the topic sentences. Topic sentences often contain linking words but never assume that a sentence with a linking word is a topic sentence. Always test the topic sentence. The sentences which follow the topic sentence should develop the topic in some way. Sentences which go in a new direction indicate a new topic.

We currently are introducing an expensive new telephone system into the company (**topic sentence**). After long discussion, we decided to buy the new system despite the initial extra cost. We made our decision by establishing a telephone committee which we created last year. The committee has been meeting once a month to evaluate our situation and to establish our needs as a business. The new telephone system will cost the company over £200,000. However, we expect the system to start paying for itself by the end of the year.

We need the new system because the system will benefit our business in a number of ways (**topic sentence**). Primarily, the old telephone system slowed the speed of our response to clients. Moreover, we often cut clients off or put clients on hold. Furthermore, clients usually had to call back if they wanted another department. Finally, clients themselves had to call consultants who were teleworking from home.

We will introduce the new telephone system into the company in October (**topic sentence**). Although we had hoped originally to have the new system in place by June, unforeseen circumstances stopped us from achieving our goal. Two events in particular took priority over installing the new system. Firstly, the basement flooded and the company had to claim over £100,000 in damages. Secondly, the Senior Management Team decided at the last minute to host an event at this year's Management Conference in London.

We will introduce the new system gradually into the company (**topic sentence**). We will start firstly in the reception areas and then move systematically to the other floors of the building.

We decided early in the planning to break the introduction of the new system into a series of stages. We made this decision for three reasons. Firstly, a graded introduction makes the process more manageable for both the staff and the committee. Secondly, a graded introduction makes the process faster. Finally, and perhaps most importantly, a graded introduction makes the process less expensive.

The new system will cover eventually the entire company in all three of our bases in the city (**topic sentence**). We expect all members of staff at all levels in all three bases to be able to use the new system confidently. Consequently, we will train all staff members systematically before the end of September. Our goal is for everyone to be completely familiar with the new system by the time we put the system into operation in October. We will install a new telephone on every desk and in every room in the company. We also will install new phones in the homes of those members of staff who work from home more than twice a week.

A cable company which operates throughout Europe will install and maintain the new system (**topic sentence**). We chose this company after exploring four other companies, two of which were national companies. The company we chose is only slightly less expensive and will take longer in fact to install the system than the other companies. However, we felt that the people with which we worked listened to our needs; carefully considered our situation; put thought into their solution; and generally made us feel that they understood what we wanted.

Bridging exercise answers

Divide the following text into paragraphs. Remember that each paragraph should begin with a topic sentence. Remember also that no paragraph should explore more than one topic.

Start by finding and underlining the topic sentences. Topic sentences often contain linking words but never assume that a sentence with a linking word is a topic sentence. Always test the topic sentence. The sentences which follow the topic sentence should develop the topic in some way. Sentences which go in a new direction indicate a new topic.

Sales of the Captain Courage action figure have begun to drop steadily after a brilliant start to the financial year (**topic sentence**). Sales of the figure peaked in September this year at 60,000 units after a steady increase throughout the previous financial year. The September figures brought the overall sales of the figure to half-a-million units since we launched the toy in November last year. However, the sales were down to 10,000 units by December this year. Independent studies show that record sales of the electronic game Traders helped to push the sales of the action figure down.

The Marketing Team credited the initial success of the action figure to the popularity of the television show on which we based the toy (**topic sentence**). The show aired on national television at 6.00pm on Friday nights which research identified as an ideal time for the target audience. The show was number one on the ratings for the entire first season. Critics believe that the show's success was due to the appeal of leading actor Storm Majors. Majors is 6'2", has dark hair, blue eyes, and an athletic build. One critic described him as "the ideal combination of values and appearances".

The action figure was low-cost because we manufactured the toy in Asia using a revolutionary new technique (**topic sentence**). Play Things Incorporated designed the action figure which is a combination of aluminium and silicone. The company is a leading Chicago-based toy designer. The action figure has a movable aluminium armature wrapped in a flexible silicone cover. We manufactured the figure in Asia because of the high level of quality and the low cost of production. We then transported the toy to our distribution centres around the world.

Thirty per cent of the buyers were girls between the ages of nine and sixteen (**topic sentence**). Nevertheless, we had aimed the action figure primarily at boys between the ages of eight and fourteen. Bradford Consulting Agency provided us with an independent investigation which gave three reasons for the shift in the target market. Firstly, actor Storm Majors became popular unexpectedly and took part in a comprehensive publicity campaign to promote the show. Majors visited over 1,000 elementary schools during the show's first season. Observers commented on the actor's natural ease with children and his ability to give positive encouragement to both boys and girls.

Secondly, the show created complex female characters which one feminist writer described as "empowered" (**topic sentence**). The same writer went on to credit the success of the female characters to the fact that three of the show's five writers are women. Finally and most importantly, Captain Courage found a female side-kick half-way through the first season in the form of Rosa, a twelve year-old orphan girl. Sales of the action figure doubled three weeks after Rosa joined the show.

The question which now remains is whether we should suspend the production line or whether we can adapt the line for a different use (**topic sentence**). Storm Majors' decision to follow a film career has threatened the future success of the television show. The show's producers are searching now for a replacement but no television show has replaced a lead actor successfully in the past. In the meantime, Ideas Unlimited has a new television show in development. The company has offered to license the characters to us provided that we use the same production technique as we do for Captain Courage. Ideas Unlimited is a Los Angeles-based independent production company. The producers plan to develop the new series into a full-length film.

Applied exercise answers

Divide the following text into paragraphs. Remember that each paragraph should begin with a topic sentence. Remember also that no paragraph should explore more than one topic.

Start by finding and underlining the topic sentences. Topic sentences often contain linking words but never assume that a sentence with a linking word is a topic sentence. Always test the topic sentence. The sentences which follow the topic sentence should develop the topic in some way. Sentences which go in a new direction indicate a new topic.

The Retail and Private Clients Division (RPC) made a profit contribution of 40% to the overall results of the Bank (**topic sentence**). The RPC Division made the highest contribution and we attribute the increase to our decision to expand the Division's client base. In the past year, we focused more on self-employed and freelance clients and we also began to provide more financial services for small businesses. Furthermore, we increased the number of our high street branches to 1,500 which provided services to eight million clients. Finally, we focused our services on providing our clients with more personal finance products and portfolio investments.

The Corporate and Institutional Banking Division (CIB) made a profit contribution of 32% to the overall results of the Bank (**topic sentence**). In this area, our client base remained National and Multinational Companies, Public Corporations, and Commercial Real Estate Clients. The CIB Division provided customer loans of 350 billion and managed deposits of 100 billion. We also increased the credit authorities of our 15,000 staff. Moreover, we expanded our Information Technology (IT) systems. Finally, we increased our consultancy services to support companies which are undergoing difficulties. In future, we plan to focus our services more clearly on the needs of our clients to ensure better returns and higher market shares.

The Investment Banking Division (IB) made a profit contribution of 28% to the overall results of the Bank (**topic sentence**). The IB Division made the lowest contribution of the three income-earning groups. We attribute this low performance to poor results in the third quarter due to pressure in Asian financial markets. However, Emerging Markets increased business development and we also saw improvements in Structured Finance and Asset Management. Unfortunately, IB fell short of this year's targets. In future, we plan to focus more on our client's expectations of investment. Changes in the market mean that our clients expect comprehensive advice combined with efficient service. We plan to keep these areas together by integrating various parts of the Bank. We also plan to maximise our world-wide trading activities by increasing our market penetration and rearranging out internal structures to help us to meet our target levels.

We have introduced a number of changes to increase the Bank's focus on the marketplace (**topic sentence**). We have increased our services primarily in IT and IT Operations (ITO) and in the function of our staff. We have increased significantly the electronic access that our clients have to the Bank. We aim to make banking attractive and easy for our clients. The developments which we have implemented are consistent and follow a strategic plan which the Operations Management Team (OMT) have designed.

However, staff levels have been less consistent than growth at the Bank (**topic sentence**). We have to adjust the levels of our staff continually because of competition and technological changes in the workplace. We tend to keep staff whose jobs have a direct impact on our relationships with clients and we tend to cut staff in administrative roles. Furthermore, we decreased our domestic staff numbers by 10,000 last year while we increased our international staff numbers by 12,000. On the whole, our workforce dropped from 75,000 last year to 70,000 this year. These figures follow the employment trends of the last five years.

Nevertheless, we have put time and energy into developing systems for staff motivation in the Bank (**topic sentence**). We recognise that staff achievement is the foundation of the success of our business. We have placed the responsibility for human resources onto the Personnel Management Division (PMD). Staff motivation is inseparable from the development of our corporate identity and our policy of knowledge management. We see the allocation of personal responsibility to staff as a direct contribution to the achievement of our corporate targets. Last year, we introduced a remuneration policy which put our non-tariff staff onto a bonus system and we introduced a performance-related pay system. Furthermore, we invested 350 million in training and we created a part-time employment scheme for staff over 55. We found the part-time employment scheme more cost efficient than early retirement.

The shares of the Bank increased significantly in the last reporting year (**topic sentence**). The market value of the shares rose and we saw an increase in value of nearly 75%. The increase in value was related to two factors. Firstly, the market expected consolidation in the global banking industry. Secondly, the market perceives the Bank to emerge as a front runner in the EMU. The increase in value will improve also the long-term performance of the shares. The increase means that £10,000 worth of shares in 1980 were valued at nearly £85,000 at the end of last year provided that the investor had bought more shares. The total is almost twice the figure of the previous year and shows an average of a 10% annual return.

Punctuation exercise answers

Punctuate the following sentences and short paragraphs. In some cases, you may have more than one alternative. In these cases, the solutions provide a suggested answer only.

1. (Y)our appointment is on (W)ednesday 14 (A)pril 2001(.)

2. (P)lease bring the following to the meeting(:) notebooks(,) pens and diaries(.)

3. (W)e have finished repairing your car and we will deliver the car to you next week(.)

4. (T)he (E)uro(L)ink train leaves from (W)aterloo (S)tation at 2(.)00pm every day of the week except (S)unday(.)

5. (A)ll (c)onsultants will receive a laptop(,) a mobile phone and a fax machine by the end of (M)arch next year(.)

6. (E)ach (C)ountry (P)icnic (H)amper must contain the following items(:) plates(,) napkins(,) glasses(,) and knives and forks(.)

7. (T)he defendant asked (L)ata(,) who had seen the accident(,) to be a witness(.) (H)owever(,) (L)ata refused to be involved in the case(.)

8. (T)he (N)ational (A)nthropology (M)useum will represent all peoples(') traditions now since we are aiming for diversity and equality(.)

Punctuate the following sentences and short paragraphs. In some cases, you may have more than one alternative. In these cases, the solutions provide a suggested answer only.

9. (J)anet (W)hite said after coming to the exhibition(:) (")(W)hy did (I) wait so long to be a part of the project(?) (I) have so much to gain from being involved(")(.)

10. (T)he two(-)day conference will take place in (B)erlin in (O)ctober(.) (W)e hope to organise a follow(-)up conference which will take place some time in the spring(.)

11. (T)he people(')s grief and anger has grown steadily at the loss of such an important public figure(.) (P)eople expect the government to respond officially before the end of the week(.)

12. (T)he company wants to change location although the risk is considerably high(.) (C)onsequently(,) the (S)enior (M)anagement (T)eam (SMT) needs to meet next week to decide which course of action to take(.)

13. (W)illiam (B)lackall will give evidence at the trial of (J)ones (&) (J)ones v(.) (U)ngerman(.) (A) full account of (M)r (B)lackall(')s testimony is contained in (A)ppendix (C)(.) (M)r (B)lackall will appear in court on (T)hursday next week(.)

14. (T)he aircraft left the airport at five o(') clock(;) that was the last that anyone has seen of the plane since that time(.) (T)he authorities have sent out a search party to see if the team(')s specialists can find the wreckage(.)

15. (R)epresentatives from (N)ew (Y)ork(,) (M)oscow(,) (P)aris(,) (D)elhi and (L)ondon all attended (T)he (F)ourth (I)nternational (C)onference of (A)lternative (R)epresentation in (R)ome(.) (N)ext year(,) the (C)onference will take place in (B)ombay or (S)idney(.)

16. (A)ll the participants felt that the (C)oaching (S)cheme had helped them in different ways(.) (I)n particular(,) many felt that the (S)cheme had promoted self(-)confidence and self(-)reliance(.) (M)ost of the participants were interested in a follow(-)up(.)

Punctuate the following sentences and short paragraphs. In some cases, you may have more than one alternative. In these cases, the solutions provide a suggested answer only.

---

17. (W)e have decided to move the (M)en(')s (D)epartment away from the (F)ood (D)epartment(.) (T)he (C)hildren(')s (D)epartment will replace the (M)en(')s (D)epartment now(.) (H)owever(,) the (W)omen(')s (D)epartment will remain next to the (S)tationery (D)epartment(.)

---

18. (T)wenty(-)five million dollars(') worth of crops has been destroyed by the recent floods which also have destroyed one(-)tenth of all the homes in the area(.) (T)he (UN) has sent troops to help the local community to begin clearing the damage so that people can return home(.)

---

19. (W)e have performed the following procedures on the property(.) (W)e have inspected the property(;) measured the site(;) made the relevant enquiries(;) and obtained all the necessary information(.) (W)e have listed the current (E)stimate (R)ealisation (V)alue of the property in (T)able (O)ne below(.)

---

20. (T)he only evidence in support of the charges 6 (b)(,) 9 (c) and 12 (a) is (J)ohn (B)rown(')s testimony(.) (C)onsequently(,) the testimony will be unsupported(.) (H)owever(,) (J)ohn is intelligent and articulate and (I) expect that he will make an excellent witness(.) (N)evertheless(,) (I) encourage the prosecution to find an additional witness as a precaution(.)

---

21. (T)he (D)evelopment (C)ommittee has made four decisions(:) everyone must complete a (S)kills (I)nventory (F)orm(;) everyone must give their (F)orms to the (L)earning (C)oordinators by (F)riday 4 (M)ay(;) the (L)earning (C)oordinators will process all the (F)orms by the end of (S)eptember this year(;) the (C)ommittee then will publish the results by the end of the calendar year(.)

22. (W)e have decided to increase the number of high street outlets which we own by 800 units(.) (C)onsequently(,) we will need to recruit nearly 3000 new members of staff(.) (O)ur (U)rban (B)usiness (E)xpansion (R)eport contains a full breakdown of our business proposal including an account of a three(-)stage implementation process(.) (O)ur research suggests that the expansion process will take a full year to implement successfully(.)

---

23. (T)he (R)etail (D)ivision has seen a steady increase in profits over the last quarter(.) (A)nalysts have credited the (D)ivision(')s success to a number of recent acquisitions(.) (I)n particular(,) the (D)ivision has acquired two new lines of clothing both of which have sold well(.) (F)urthermore(,) the (D)ivision has launched an in(-)house magazine called (F)abrication(.) (T)he (D)ivision designed the magazine to promote the clothing and sales have doubled in the last quarter(.)

---

24. (T)he (U)rban (D)evelopment (P)roposal recognises that the six areas of the (C)ounty(,) including (M)iddlerow, represent a unique social(,) economic and cultural resource(.) (T)he regeneration and redevelopment of these areas will benefit the community in five ways(:) they will meet the development needs of small(-)business people(;) they will maintain investment from larger companies(;) they will enhance the quality of life for the locals(;) they will sustain the economy(;) and finally(,) they will relieve development pressures on the countryside(.)

Style and tone exercise answers

Essential exercise
answers Change the style and tone of the following sentences where
necessary. The solutions are suggested answers.

---

1. I need this proposal by Thursday. Are you able to help me?

   ---

2. Please contact me on 0171 645 3426 if you want to discuss
   the supplies.

   ---

3. Please contact me on 0171 546 6243 if you have any other
   questions.

   ---

4. I need you to return the forms to me by Tuesday.

   ---

5. I need this work done by Wednesday next week. Are you able
   to do the work in that time?

   ---

6. Thank you for your letter of 20 August 2002. Unfortunately,
   we no longer make the product you ordered. Consequently, I
   have enclosed a catalogue for you to consider an alternative.

Bridging exercise
answers Change the style and tone of the following sentences where
necessary. The solutions are suggested answers.

---

7. I feel that I have answered your questions as completely as I
   am able. Furthermore, I have made my decision and I am in
   a position where I cannot reverse my choice. Consequently, I
   must ask you please to call this number no more.

   ---

8. I have a problem with the printer and I estimate that the
   problem will take at least a day to fix. I will contact you
   tomorrow to tell you how close I am to solving the problem.

   ---

9. Thank you for bringing your car to the garage. Unfortunately,
   we have had to order the parts which you need. As a result,
   your car will be ready in two days' time.

10. We need the consultants to give us at least two days' lead time when we produce work for clients. We realise that this lead time is not always possible because of the nature of the industry. However, more lead time will make a great difference in the quality of the work which we produce.

11. We made a mistake with your order. Consequently, we have sent you a replacement. Please contact John on 0171 546 7387 if the replacement is unsuitable.

12. The majority of the men in the group appeared to have difficulty in addressing emotional issues. Four out of the five men preferred to focus on the processes of management rather than focussing on emotions.

Applied exercise answers

Change the style and tone of the following sentences where necessary. The solutions are suggested answers.

13. I am sorry that I was unable to return your e-mail sooner. Would you like to tell me now how I can help you.

14. We are all responsible for helping clients who call the organisation. Moreover, we are all responsible for letting other people know where we are when we leave our desks. People need to know where we are so that they can answer the phone if we are unavailable.

15. I need you to complete the report by Monday. Furthermore, I need the report to be perfect since the client is one of our major accounts. I realise that you will have to change your work plans to finish the report. Consequently, I am willing to give you all the support which you need to get the work right.

16. I am sorry to hear that your father passed away recently. I hope that you and your family are receiving all the support which you need. I realise that you are under emotional stress at the moment. Nevertheless, I need you to make a decision. The project is starting next week and I would like you to be a part of the team. Please take some time to consider your situation and let me know what kind of support you will need to be involved in the project.

17. Please be punctual for the presentations. Speaking to groups of people is stressful and you put the speaker under additional pressure when you arrive late. We welcome your involvement in our work and we ask you to be respectful of our efforts.

18. Consultants have been late with their expenses for the past six months. As a result, we are unable to calculate accurately the costs of the department. Consequently, we have decided to charge a 5% fee to consultants who claim their expenses later than the 25th of each month. Please contact us to discuss any exceptional situations.

G Bibliography

The Economist Style Guide, The Economist Books Ltd, 1993

Emotional Intelligence, Daniel Goleman, Bloomsbury Publishing Plc, 1996

The Oxford English Grammar, Sidney Greenbaum, Oxford University Press, 1996

Practical English Usage, Michael Swan, Oxford University Press, 1996

Suggested reading list for Writing Skills courses

General *The Complete Plain Words*, Sir Ernest Gowers, Penguin, 1962

Writing at Work, Alan Barker, The Industrial Society, 1999*

Words *Getting to Grips with Vocabulary*, Catherine Hilton and Margaret Hyder, Letts Educational, 1992

Dictionary of Troublesome Words, Bill Bryson, Penguin, 1987

Good reading *The State of the Language*, Philip Howard, Penguin, 1986

Mother Tongue, Bill Bryson, Penguin, 1991

The Language Instinct, Stephen Pinker, Penguin Books Ltd, 1995

*Available direct from The Industrial Society.